7 80

Furniture Restoration

057

Furniture Restoration

KEVIN JAN BONNER

GUILD OF MASTER CRAFTSMAN PUBLICATIONS LTD

First published 1996 by
Guild of Master Craftsman Publications Ltd,
166 High Street, Lewes,
East Sussex BN7 1XU

ISBN 1 86108 012 3

This edition is a revised and condensed version of
Furniture Restoration and Repair for Beginners,
published in 1994 by Guild of Master Craftsman
Publications Ltd.

Designed by Ian Hunt Design

Set in Meridien

Printed in Hong Kong by H&Y Printing Ltd
Colour Separation by Global Colour (Malaysia)

CONTENTS

INTRODUCTION

USING THIS BOOK

The information in this guide is the result of my listening and responding to the needs and questions of students attending my furniture restoration classes over many years, and I have deliberately kept the language as free as possible from technical terms and jargon.

Everything covered in the following pages is well within the expertise of those with little or no DIY experience, while at the same time containing information about processes which are in common use among seasoned professionals.

The book progresses through the essential steps of furniture restoration: tools, equipment, how to stay safe and healthy as you work, identifying finishes, repairing finishes, fixing and staining, followed by common finishing techniques and their properties, such as the ease and speed of application, flammability, toxicity and durability. This will enable you to judge which finish suits your particular project and circumstances.

'MASS PRODUCTION' LACQUERS

Because they are more suited to commercial application, I have deliberately not included a chapter devoted to this family of modern finishes. (By 'modern' I mean post World War Two.) However, you may wish to explore their use in restoration further once you have gained a good grounding of experience in restoration techniques, in which case I hope you will find the following brief overview helpful.

Furniture manufacturers can choose from a wide range of lacquer finishes, such as cellulose lacquers, polyester lacquers, two-part lacquers, precatalysed lacquers and acid-cured lacquers. All these finishes are designed to be sprayed on to furniture in a factory environment, and are quick-drying and hard wearing, being scratch-, alcohol-, water- and heat-resistant.

Types of finish range from a very thick, high-gloss finish (used on pianos and bar tops, for example), to thin, matt sealers which are used on office and other utilitarian furniture. The care of these finishes is very simple – all that is needed is the occasional wipe over with a damp cloth.

These finishes, despite all their wonderful attributes, are not recommended for the home restorer or DIY enthusiast because they contain very powerful and volatile chemicals. This requires that they be applied only in a specialized workshop or factory which is equipped with extraction fans and spray booths. Application of this kind of finish also requires the wearing of special masks and breathing apparatus.

Some finish manufacturers have produced a variation of the modern lacquer finish for the DIY market, designed to be applied using a brush. They produce a very hard, durable finish but also emit a very strong chemical smell during application. If you wish to try such a finish, I would advise you to contact a suitable supplier, purchase a trial size and rigorously follow the manufacturer's instructions.

TOOLS, EQUIPMENT AND WORKING ENVIRONMENT

The tools and equipment required to restore furniture are minimal, inexpensive and many are to be found in the average home. Most of the suggested materials are available from DIY stores. I have presumed you will be working in a space set aside at home, in a small workshop, the garage or the garden, and that the furniture to be restored is intact and not in need of cabinetmaking skills to make a new leg or a replacement drawer.

APPROACHES

It is useful to bear the following in mind before embarking on any specific project:

GO WITH THE FLOW

First, if you find yourself saddled with an impossible task (sometimes you will not realize this until you are halfway through a project), there may be an alternative approach you can adopt which will turn the problem into an opportunity. For example, if the cabinet you are restoring is covered by black ink stains, consider ebonizing or painting it rather than trying to remove the stains in order to French polish the piece. Allow the furniture to speak to you; it will often tell you the best type of finish for it.

THINK AHEAD

Always think ahead. Over-enthusiastic students often charge on with a project without stopping to think about the function of the finished piece. Consider the use to which you will put your furniture before investing your time restoring it in a particular way. If you intend a piece to be a gift for the Prince of Wales, a different approach is called for than if you intend to use it to cover a damp patch in your spare room. Think ahead.

BLEMISH INTO AN EYESORE

Be wary of turning a small and perfectly acceptable blemish into an eyesore. This is a common occurrence among beginners, who, lacking furniture requiring serious restoration, try instead to remove minor scratches and end up with a piece looking far, far worse than it did to begin with.

If you are a beginner, start with a piece that requires complete stripping, and remember that it is the small things which often require the most skill and experience to restore correctly.

WHEN TO STOP

In the same way as it is important to know what to restore, you also need to know how much to restore it. That is, when to stop. If you have spent weeks stripping, staining, fixing and refinishing a piece it is often hard to know when to stop. You find yourself looking for minor blemishes so that you can make the piece just that little bit nearer perfection. The results of such tinkering can be disastrous, and in extreme cases, particularly fussy craftspeople have been known to strip the finish off completely and start all over again.

Remember, a certain amount of wear and tear is essential to old furniture. In the trade it is known as 'character', and you must learn to value it, as it is what makes your furniture unique.

1
WHAT TO RESTORE

POSSIBLE SOURCES

The most common source for restoration projects is the would-be restorer's own home. As I have already mentioned, don't take on anything too ambitious (or, if you are a complete beginner, dear to your heart in any way!). If you have nothing at home which needs restoration, there are a number of places you can look. Some suggestions are listed below. As the list progresses, specific pieces will be easier to find but at the same time progressively more expensive to obtain.

- Skips, rubbish bins and rubbish dumps.
- Car boot sales and jumble sales.
- Market traders and antique bric-a-brac fairs.
- Local papers, garage sales and house clearances.
- Junk shops.
- Small auction houses (for household effects).
- Low to middle market antique shops.
- Antique fairs.
- Large auction houses (for antiques and collectables).
- Upmarket antique shops.

Fig 1.1 Junk shops are ideal places to pick up suitable projects for restoration.

I favour junk shops the most, as here you can achieve a reasonable balance between the cost and the time spent looking for a suitable project (see Fig 1.1).

(see Fig 1.1)

WHAT TO AVOID

If you are a beginner, try to exercise caution and avoid a first project which will overstretch your ability. Do not choose a piece if it:

- is valuable, financially or sentimentally.
- is intricately carved (awkward and frustrating to strip).
- has barley twist legs (difficult to strip) (see Fig 1.2).
- is too heavy to lift.
- has any part of it missing.
- has a lot of damaged or missing veneer.
- involves removal (rather than protection) of upholstery.

Fig 1.2 Barley twist legs on a drop-leaf table. Avoid such features on your first few projects if you intend to strip the piece, as the process will be very time consuming.

It is also wise to avoid complex pieces which have a French polish finish. While French polish is one of the easiest finishes to remove, it is not the easiest to apply, so, if you are intent on practising your French polishing skills, choose a small table with a flat top and plain uncarved legs to begin with.

Conversely, one of the hardest finishes to remove is a properly applied paint finish on open-grained wood (such as oak or elm), which will have involved primer, undercoat and topcoat. Such finishes are extremely common, and can have you tearing your hair out in frustration. Avoid them at all costs, unless they have been applied over French polish. The French polish prevents the paint from adhering to open-grained bare wood, making it easier to remove (see Fig 1.3). Test such finishes first

Fig 1.3 Paint applied over French polish is easy to remove. Sometimes it will already be chipped in places, as here, making identification of the finish very easy.

to find out how hard the project is likely to be; simply scratch the surface with a penknife to see if there is a French-polished surface underneath. If not, look for an easier project to start off with.

WHAT TO BUY

Look out for solid woods. Anything made of solid wood, as opposed to chipboard, and has lasted 50 years will continue to last. Pre-war solid oak furniture is widely available, well made and low-priced, and looks superb when properly restored and refinished.

Furniture constructed from plywood is by no means inferior however. As long as the veneers that comprise the plywood are in good condition and not bubbling up, then the piece will be both robust and practical, well worth restoring and refinishing.

A good starting project is a simple chair, which will be easy to strip, as would a small, flat-topped table (see Fig 1.4). Such pieces are widely available in junk shops, and will serve a practical purpose when your work is done.

BEFORE YOU BUY

Bear in mind the following before buying a piece:

▌ Have I got adequate space to work on it?
▌ Does the piece need to be delivered? Does the shop deliver?
▌ Will I be able to start work straight away?
▌ If not, do I have storage space?
▌ What finish will it need?
▌ How long will such a project take me?
▌ Do I have the time to spare?

However alien to the British culture it may be, do try and haggle. You will be amazed at the positive results of persistence on your pocket! Other tips based on my own experiences which may help to improve your purchasing power are:

- Shop on a weekday if you can; trade will be slower, there will be more time to bargain and the trader may be more open to making a deal.
- Make friends with the trader; they can prove to be a very useful ally in your present or future searches, as they regularly attend auctions and house-clearance sales, and may be willing to keep an eye out for the piece you are looking for at the price you wish to pay.

Regardless of your haggling powers, it is comforting and I hope encouraging to remember that most second-hand furniture is vastly under-priced. For example, if you were to buy a good, solid second-hand oak table from a junk shop and then have the same item made to the same quality by a present-day craftsperson, the price difference would be phenomenal. Choose your second-hand furniture with care and you will end up with a bargain every time.

Fig 1.4 A simple chair or a small, flat-topped table are excellent first projects.

2
WORKSPACE, TOOLS AND MATERIALS

WORKSPACE

Once you have found a suitable piece of furniture, you must find a suitable space in which to work. This will depend on a number of factors, but you should consider the following points when choosing.

- Your workspace should be large enough to place your project in the middle and leave enough room to walk around it. Some projects may need an old table or bench to raise the piece off the ground to a comfortable working height.
- It is helpful to have an area away from the project where you can place materials, tools and other equipment without them getting knocked over or being in your way.
- If you are working in the garage, shed or workshop, try to limit the amount of dust. Running a vacuum cleaner over the workplace before commencing can be helpful.
- Try to ensure the workplace is sheltered from air movement. Breezes and draughts can whip up small dust clouds which will undoubtedly find their way on to and into your finishes as they dry.
- Plan to have the use of the space for at least a few days. Depending on the process involved you may need to leave your project overnight to dry undisturbed.

Having said all this, it is possible to do restoration work in your kitchen as long as you are careful not to get one set of ingredients mixed up with another and are willing to be flexible.

LIGHTING

Ideally, there should be some form of natural light. It is not commonly recognized that natural light, even on a cloudy day in the middle of winter, is many times stronger than artificial interior lighting. As such, it will illuminate and expose much more effectively. If you want to see the true colour of a piece of wood or a stain, always view it in natural light. This also applies to inspecting surfaces for blemishes, applying finishes and colour-matching.

Always check your work in natural daylight. As a rule, if it looks passable in daylight, it will look magnificent in artificial light.

Be aware also of the problem of 'reflected colour' whereby the colour of one thing is altered by it 'taking on' the colour of surrounding objects.

If you work at night or in the evenings, as I often do, invest in some extra lighting for your workspace. This will be less tiring on the eyes and provide a much safer environment. Strip lighting is ideal.

THE IDEAL WORKSPACE

My favourite place for restoring is the garden. This has a number of practical benefits: the lighting is unsurpassed, on a still day there is no dust, ventilation is excellent and there is more than enough room. Obviously use of outdoor space relies on favourable weather (i.e. dry and still). Windblown matter can be disastrous at certain phases of a project (such as varnishing), but a light breeze during stripping will be beneficial in helping to dispel the noxious fumes.

Try to avoid direct sunlight if you can as it can adversely affect the wood and cause some finishes to dry too quickly, making them hard to apply. Low temperatures can also affect the drying and application

qualities of some finishes. The effect of these conditions on each finish is addressed in the relevant chapter.

If you are working indoors, be sure to protect carpets, wallpaper and soft furnishings, allow sufficient ventilation, and stick to the safety checklist printed on page 16 at all times.

TOOLS

You do not need a vast array of tools to restore furniture. The following tools and materials should be purchased only as and when they become necessary.

SCRAPERS

You will need a selection of these for removing old finishes. Some should be shop-bought (costing a few pounds each), others can be home-made from old kitchen knives, lollipop sticks and old craft knife blades, as and when you need them (see Fig 2.1).

BRUSHES

You will also need a selection of old and new decorator's brushes of various sizes. The use to which a brush is put dictates the quality of brush required, and this is indicated in each chapter as you go along. However, it is worth mentioning

Fig 2.1 A selection of scrapers.

Fig 2.2 A selection of decorator's brushes. When restoring furniture, even the most dilapidated brushes will have their use, particularly when stripping, applying oil, or staining.

Fig 2.3 Artists' brushes are required for more delicate work such as painting in graining effects.

here (before it is too late) that any brushes you may have left over from the decorating which you are about to throw away because they are ruined by ineffective cleaning are ideal for stripping (see Fig 2.2).

You will also need smaller artists' brushes to paint-in graining effects and textures when fixing and camouflaging with colour; such brushes are available from any artists' supply shop (see Fig 2.3).

RAGS

You will need an endless supply of absorbent rags for applying stains, cleaning off, wiping your hands, applying finishes, cleaning up spillages and crying into if things go wrong. A supply of old newspapers is also useful for protecting floors, upholstery and walls.

CLAMPS

When re-gluing you may need wood clamps to hold things together while they dry, and to squeeze joints as tightly as possible. These can be expensive, so only buy them as you need them (see Fig 2.4 and page 54).

Clamps can also be hired, and even home-made. The easiest to make is known as the windlass or tourniquet clamp. At its simplest this is a piece of string or thin rope looped around the furniture; the slack is removed by twisting a piece of wood into the string to tighten. Try several of these on your furniture and see if that cures the problem before investing in 'proper' clamps.

ABRASIVES

ABRASIVE PAPER

A bewildering array of abrasive papers are available on the DIY shelf (see Fig 2.5). All you need to start off with is one or two sheets of fine-grade sandpaper for smoothing down wood surfaces such as rough table tops before refinishing, and the same amount of 600 grit wet-or-dry. This is also known as silicone carbide paper and is used for rubbing down finishes between coats. It is a much finer grade of abrasive paper than ordinary sandpapers, and if it becomes clogged it can be washed out in the sink with soap and running water, therefore lasting longer than ordinary sandpaper.

WIRE WOOL

You will need some wire wool (also known as steel wool) in two or three different grades: fine, medium and coarse. It is wise to wear protective gloves when using this material as it has a nasty habit of dispensing invisible steel splinters into the fingers during use.

Fig 2.4 A selection of clamps used by furniture restorers. As with many of the tools you will need, they are best bought on a buy-as-you-need basis.

Fig 2.5 A selection of abrasives.

SUEDE BRUSH

You will need a suede brush for stripping complicated areas such as mouldings and carvings, and such brushes can be bought from shoe repairers and supermarkets. See Chapter 7 for more information.

GLUES

POLYVINYL ACETATE

More often referred to as PVA, this is the most commonly available wood glue, produced by a number of manufacturers. It is inexpensive, water washable and easy to use. It is white in colour but dries clear, and is available in indoor and outdoor formulations. It is also completely safe in normal use (see Fig 2.6). For ease of use I decant PVA into a pot and apply it with a spatula.

This glue will cover 90% of the absolute beginner's needs, and works best when gluing closely fitting joints. It is not so effective with loose-fitting joints, which unfortunately tend to occur rather a lot with old furniture.

Another drawback is that PVA can sometimes be too effective. For example, imagine you are ready to reassemble a chair; all the joints fit nicely together so you choose PVA, but the problem occurs when you have to pull open a joint which you have just glued so that you can fit in another section of the chair, or need

Fig 2.6 PVA glue, here decanted into a jar and clearly labelled. Although marketed by several manufacturers and in a variety of formulations, it always looks the same.

for the mix are always supplied but I prefer a simpler method. Mix a spoonful of the powder with a few drops of water and stir. If the mixture is too thick add a little more water, if too thin add a little more powder, and so on until you have a creamy consistency.

Cascamite dries clear to a glass-like hardness by chemical reaction. It begins to go sticky about 20 minutes after application, allowing plenty of time to make any adjustments or corrections to your assembly procedure.

Cascamite can cause dermatitis if it makes contact with the skin, so be careful. You should also avoid breathing in the powder, for obvious reasons. Cascamite can be obtained from timber and builders' merchants and trade supply houses.

to take it apart and begin again because you have made a mistake. Unfortunately, the better the fit of the joint the quicker PVA works, and in some cases it may adhere immediately, leaving you completely stuck!

UREA-FORMALDEHYDE GLUE

This does not act quite so rapidly as PVA and is hence an ideal solution to the problem outlined above. The most common make in the UK is called Cascamite, which comes in the form of a white powder which is then mixed with water. Instructions

Disadvantages of urea-formaldehyde glue

- Not as readily available as PVA.
- Less economic than PVA (surplus not used must be discarded).
- More expensive than PVA.

Advantages

- Copes with those tasks not appropriate for PVA.
- Extremely weatherproof.

TRADITIONAL SCOTCH GLUE

Also known as hide or animal glue, this has some benefits but is notoriously difficult to use. It is heat-sensitive, and so is heated in a pot to the required temperature, and in use it cools quickly and contracts slightly, pulling the pieces of wood or joints firmly together. As this often occurs within seconds there is no need for clamps or long drying times before moving on to the next stage. In the hands of a skilled craftsperson, heavenly things can be achieved; in the hands of an absolute beginner all hell can be let loose. The use of this glue requires a certain amount of skill, and, because of the need for heat, can be dangerous when (or if) it is surrounded by flammable chemicals.

However, there are some jobs for which no other glue is suitable, such as fixing glue blocks to the backs of mirrors (see page 66), or where the actual shape of the items to be joined prevents the use of any other type of glue, such as the ears of a cabriole leg, which are difficult to clamp together (see Fig 2.7).

It is also moisture-sensitive, and so will often fail if furniture is subjected to damp (a common occurrence). Most pre-war furniture will have used some form of this glue in its manufacture.

Scotch glue can be unstuck if the need arises by wrapping hot cloths around a joint or in difficult cases drilling a small hole and injecting hot water. This is one of the positive

Fig 2.7 A cabriole leg. If the pieces of wood on either side of the top of the leg (known as the ears) come unstuck, they can be difficult to stick back into place without the aid of traditional scotch glue.

aspects of scotch glue, greatly valued by restorers of antique pieces, because it means their repairs are reversible.

GLUE FILM

This comes in a roll, backed with paper, and is used for applying and repairing veneers. It is heat-sensitive and can be tacked to the back of a veneer, then ironed on to the ground work. This makes working with veneers extremely simple. It is inexpensive but can only be bought from specialist suppliers.

3
HEALTH AND SAFETY

COMMON SENSE

Happily, many of the dangerous situations that you will encounter with furniture restoration are obvious and subject to common sense. For example, if you are finishing a piece of furniture with a highly flammable finish, it makes sense not to smoke a pipe at the same time.

Some dangers are not quite so self-evident, and it is these to which I draw your attention now, and will continue to emphasize throughout this book.

ACCIDENTS

These are by their nature unexpected. You do not expect to fall off a ladder or trip over a wire; if you did, you wouldn't. There is no way to predict your own accident but there are ways to lessen the likelihood of an accident happening in the first place. Adopting and maintaining safe working practices, and being aware of what to do should something go wrong will drastically reduce the chance of an accident.

What follows is a safety checklist of more general but extremely important safety points. Abide by them and you will go a long way to achieving and maintaining an accident-free workplace.

SAFETY CHECKLIST

Before starting work, think 'safety', and mentally go through this list. Every time you come back from a break, repeat this process. It may help to photocopy this list and pin it up in a prominent position in your workplace.

- Do not eat, drink or smoke while working.
- Clear your work surface every half-an-hour or so of any unwanted tools or materials.
- Always replace the lids of containers as soon as you have finished using them and wipe up any spills straight away.
- Keep children, pets and interfering adults out of your workplace and minimize any kind of interruption. Before you begin work, take the phone off the hook and hang up a 'do not

disturb' sign. Make sure there is nothing left in the oven or on the boil (accidents don't just happen in the workshop).

- Ensure your project is at a comfortable height to work on at all times.
- Keep the floor clear of hazards such as electrical cables, debris or slippery surfaces.
- Guard against fire; many woodfinishing chemicals are flammable. Always have a bowl of water, a fire blanket and a fire extinguisher to hand.
- Keep a well-stocked first-aid kit within easy reach.
- Label any preparations you make yourself clearly and keep all poisonous and dangerous chemicals in a locked cabinet.
- If you are about to try something which you feel you need assistance with, get assistance. Your concerns about trying it on your own are far more likely to be justified than not.
- Only use 'strong' chemicals in a well-ventilated area, and always abide by the instructions provided with them.
- Always take any health problems you may have into consideration. Particularly significant illnesses are any form of lung complaint, skin problems, any form of back injury, and tennis elbow (repetitive strain injury to arms and wrists).
- Always wear protective clothing: mask to protect the mouth and nose from dust, earmuffs or plugs to protect against noise from power tools if used, gloves for the hands and visors or goggles for the eyes and face.

4
HOW TO IDENTIFY FINISHES

In time, identification of finishes will become second nature to you, and you will be able to tell some finishes just by looking at them. Often the style and age of furniture or the way the finish has deteriorated will give you an indication as to its nature.

There is a series of simple experiments you can carry out to identify a finish. Before you begin, if the piece looks dirty and waxy, give the surface you intend to test a thorough clean with white spirit.

■ Spill a small drop of methylated spirit on to an inconspicuous corner and scratch the moistened area gently with your index fingernail (see Fig 4.1). If

Fig 4.1 Applying the fingernail test to a French polish finish.

it is French polish the finish will soften within 15 seconds and some gunge will be noticeable under your fingernail. Furniture produced before 1945 is likely to be French polished.

▌ If the finish takes longer to soften (within two minutes) and looks as if it has been applied with a brush it is probably a spirit varnish.

▌ If the finish fails to soften, rub a similar area with a fingertip of cloth soaked in white spirit. If the finish goes dull and eventually rubs back to bare wood, then you are dealing with a wax type finish.

▌ If the surface is cleaned by this action and becomes a little sticky, it is likely to be an oil-based finish.

▌ If the surface is unaffected by either of these methods, it is likely to be a more modern (post 1945) finish. Try a drop of chemical stripper (see Chapter 7). If the finish softens, bubbles up, thickens and looks as if it may have been applied with an amateur brush it is likely to be polyurethane.

▌ If this fails and the finish appears to be sprayed on, try a cellulose chemical stripper (available from car accessory shops).

Remember that furniture may have been subjected to more than one finish in its life, each lying over the other; wax over French polish is very common as is wax over an oil finish.

Painted furniture is usually obvious, but bear in mind the different types of paint: oil and emulsion. Oil is easily softened by a chemical stripper, whereas emulsion will need to be scraped off.

5
HOW TO REPAIR FINISHES

If you have decided to strip a piece of furniture, stop! A restorer should always try the least invasive techniques first before moving on to more aggressive methods. Stripping and refinishing should always be the last resort.

Hence it is wise to experiment on the finish with some of the following recipes before finally stripping. This will give you a chance to experiment with various remedies without the fear of making a mistake.

This chapter begins with the simplest repairing remedies and proceeds through the common problems which occur with old furniture. Many remedies then direct you to other parts of the book for more information.

WHITE MARKS

These are very very common, especially on French polished surfaces, and are caused by moisture being absorbed into the finish. If the mark is ring-shaped it is likely that a plant stand, vase or glass is the culprit. If the mark is an amorphous cloudiness it may have been caused

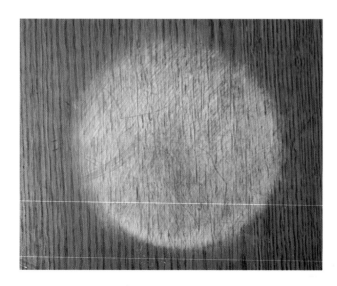

Fig 5.1 White marks such as this, caused by moisture on the surface of the finish, are very common on old furniture.

by moisture in the air, a damp atmosphere or even a damp cloth or spillages being allowed to sit on the surface (see Fig 5.1).

First things first: establish what kind of finish you are dealing with (see Chapter 4). If, as is likely, you identify the finish as French polish, there are a number of possible options.

RUBBING COMPOUND

First I suggest you try rubbing compound, obtainable from all car accessory shops.

With a fingertip of damp cloth, gently rub the compound into the white mark. In 85% of cases you will see the mark slowly disappear (see Fig 5.2).

Other abrasive creams can be used to achieve the same result:

burnishing cream, metal polish, bath-scouring compounds and even toothpaste can all be used to good effect. The traditional Victorian recipe was a paste made from cigar or cigarette ash and single cream or cooking oil, which makes a very fine abrasive paste.

If the surface in question is very shiny and you use a slightly over-coarse abrasive, you may find you are left with a dull patch where the white mark used to be. The reverse can occur if you work on a matt surface with a fine abrasive, which can leave a shiny patch. It is only by trial and error that you will be able to match the abrasive to the surface, but the rule is, the coarser the compound the duller the finish.

Be careful not to rub too hard or too fast as this can abrade away a

Fig 5.2 Rubbing compound or a similar abrasive cream is extremely effective at removing white marks, as you can see here, where the job is halfway to completion.

very thin or old deteriorated coating of French polish. If the polish is too far gone then it needs to be renewed in any case. That is, the area will have to be repolished (see Chapter 15) or the whole piece stripped and restored from scratch (see Chapter 7).

AMMONIA

If you suspect the finish to be thin you may wish to try the ammonia remedy. However, ammonia is an extremely powerful and pungent chemical, and in undiluted form gives off strong caustic vapours and will burn the skin if spilled. Always use with great care, and avoid its use altogether if you have respiratory problems. Use this chemical in a well-ventilated area, preferably out of doors and well away from children and animals.

Ammonia can be obtained from the chemist, and the process is then as follows:

1   Dilute the ammonia to a 50/50 mix with water (this makes it an awful lot safer to work with, but you should still wear gloves).
2   Working slowly and purposefully, rub the solution into the white mark using a soft cloth.
3   As you work be very wary of any adverse reactions such as a darkening in the colour of the wood. If that happens you will have to strip the surface back to bare wood and then stain it all the same colour and refinish!
4   If the finish starts to soften, the mixture is too strong, so add more water.

If all goes well you should see the mark slowly disappear before your eyes.

REMEDIES FOR OTHER FINISHES

If you've tried both the above remedies and still don't have a result, you have probably misdiagnosed the type of finish and a slightly different approach will be called for.

POLYURETHANE OR CELLULOSE LACQUER

If it is a hard type of finish it is sure to be either polyurethane varnish or some form of cellulose lacquer. In this case all you have to do is rub a little harder with the abrasive compound or use a coarser compound. If the mark still persists you must resort to rubbing the compound with fine wire wool. Don't worry if this creates a dull mark, as the area can always be re-shined with a finer grade compound once the white mark has gone.

JAPANESE LACQUER

On Japanese lacquer, moisture marks tend to be an orangey yellow colour and can be removed using the ammonia method. Don't use any abrasive compound on this finish, as you run the risk of damaging or removing altogether the raised picture sections of the lacquer work.

WAX FINISH

White marks on wax finishes are easily removed by lightly swabbing the area with a thin liquid wax mix and polishing (see Chapter 13).

OIL FINISH

Try rubbing in a thinned oil mix (see Chapter 14).

BLACK MARKS

There are three types of black mark you may come across on furniture.

INK STAINS

These are commonly found on any furniture associated with writing. The ink is the old fountain or quill pen type and is a close cousin to the spirit stains furniture restorers use to stain wood (see Chapter 12). Such ink stains often only penetrate as far as the finish and can therefore be removed with the finish if you are stripping.

If not (i.e. the stain is superficial and the finish is thick), the stain may be removable by rubbing with abrasive creams such as those mentioned above. However, I should emphasize that if the stains penetrate through to the wood, then their complete removal will necessitate stripping the finish and scraping the surface of the wood with a chisel or a craft knife blade (see Fig 5.3). With luck the problem can be scratched away by this method, and providing you don't have to scratch too deeply the colour of the wood will also be preserved.

BURNS

Black marks are also caused by cigarettes and cigars left on the edge of table tops or rolling out of ashtrays unnoticed. Such marks are easily identified by their shape and position.

Black marks caused by burns necessitate scraping the burnt fibres out of the surface of the wood with a sharp-edged implement, such as a craft knife or the tip of a sharp chisel. This will take care of the burn but may result in an unsightly depression (hopefully on the wood, not in the restorer on seeing the results). If this is the case, Chapter 11 on fillers provides the remedy.

REMOVING MARKS WITH A CHISEL

Fig 5.3 Removing a black mark from an oak piano lid using a sharp chisel.

CHEMICAL STAINS

Black marks can also be caused by chemical stains. Tannic acid naturally occurs in woods such as oak, chestnut and mahogany, and when these woods come into contact with water and some metals (such as metal pans or vases), a chemical reaction can take place: tannic acid attacks the metal and a black stain results. Such stains can penetrate deep into the fibres of the wood and leave a black ring mark. The method for removing such stains is exactly the same as that for ink stains.

SANDING

You can also remove black marks by sanding, providing you're not concerned with the antique value of the piece. Such a process will remove a fraction of a millimetre off the surface of the wood baring fresh, unpainted, and hopefully unmarked wood. As a result of this, when sanding areas such as table tops you may find that the top ends up a lighter colour than the rest of the table. In such a case the top will have to be stained to match the legs (see Chapter 12).

If you decide to sand, be sure to do so with the grain, finishing off with the finest grade of paper you can get (see Fig 5.4). There are a number of power tools which will make the sanding process easier, such as a power sander (see Fig 5.5), but hand sanding will still be required in awkward areas.

Both hand and power sanding generate a lot of dust, so always be sure to wear a suitable dust mask

Fig 5.4 When sanding by hand, always rub in the direction of the grain, never across it, and use a fine grade paper.

Fig 5.5 A power sander will make sanding large areas quicker and easier, but hand sanding will still be required for the more awkward areas.

and any other protection you deem necessary such as hats and glasses.

I suggest you try some of the other remedies before sanding; they are less labour intensive and if they work will produce a better result. Regard sanding as a last resort.

BLEACHING

Black marks can also be removed by bleaching. This is a complicated process and the behaviour of the bleach, the stain and the various chemicals in the wood make it an unpredictable one also. It is not a method I would recommend to the absolute beginner. If you really want to give it a go, then I recommend buying a proprietary brand of bleach and following the instructions provided with great care.

DENTS

Dents and depressions are another very common ailment afflicting furniture of all ages. If you imagine the microscopic composition of wood as being like a bunch of straws, when the wood is dented these straws become compressed, leaving an unsightly blemish. All you have to do to reinflate the compressed fibres is apply a cotton wool poultice. Simply soak some cotton wool with tap water, mould it into the size and shape of the dent, and lay it on the surface of the wood (see Fig 5.6). Monitor progress about once an hour – really nasty dents need to have the poultice sealed with 2in (51mm) wide packing tape to stop the cotton wool drying out, and be left overnight (see Fig 5.7).

Fig 5.6 Applying a cotton wool 'poultice' to a dent will help to reinflate the compressed fibres of the wood.

The process can be accelerated if you wish, by touching the tip of a hot iron on to the wet cotton wool. This forces the moisture deep into the fibres of the wood thus speeding up the process. This operation is repeated until the dent is removed.

If this method fails it is likely that some fibres of wood have been removed at the time the piece received the knock. Replacement rather than reinflation is therefore the answer, using filler (see Chapter 11).

Fig 5.7 Nasty dents will need the poultices to be sealed with packing tape to prevent the cotton wool drying out too quickly, so that they can be left to work overnight.

DRAWBACKS OF THE COTTON WOOL METHOD

- On an unstripped piece, the finish must be broken down to allow moisture penetration. On an unbroken finish you can achieve this by piercing the finish with a pin or craft knife blade.
- A French polish finish will suffer from a white mark as a result. Once the area is completely dry this can be removed using the process described on page 21.
- Bare-stripped wood may suffer from an over-inflation of fibres, leaving them proud of the surface. Rubbing down will remove some patina and leave a lighter area which may need to be patched in with stains. To avoid such problems, keep checking the work every hour! Prevention is always better than cure.

SCRATCHES AND GOUGES

These ailments are very common in furniture, and they vary from very fine scratches and abrasions to the deep gouges of the schoolboy penknife.

A filler is usually the answer (see Chapter 11), or if your project is French polished the antiquikstrip process followed by repolishing may also be a solution (see Chapter 8).

DETERIORATED FINISHES

It is usually best to strip badly deteriorated finishes and start again, but every now and again you may find a finish which is not bad enough to require stripping but too bad to live with. Antiquikstrip is once again an option here (see Chapter 8).

REVIVERS

Revivers can have an amazing rejuvenating effect on old and neglected furniture, and they involve very little expenditure in time, effort or money.

FRENCH POLISH REVIVER

This is the most common type of reviver and is made up as follows:

1 Mix equal quantities of white spirit, methylated spirit and boiled linseed oil.
2 Shake vigorously to achieve a creamy yellow mixture (see Fig 5.8).

Allowed to stand, the mixture will separate out into its constituent parts, and so should always be shaken before use.

Fig 5.8 Revivers will separate into their constituent parts after they have been left standing, so always remember to shake them well before use, giving the yellow, creamy mixture seen here.

To apply, dip a cotton cloth into the reviver and rub it into small areas with a polishing action. Then polish off with a clean cloth. Be sure not to leave any residue on the surface as it contains methylated spirit which will have a softening

effect on French polish if left too long. Alternatively, decant the mixture into a garden-spray bottle, spray on to the surface and immediately polish off.

The function of the methylated spirit is to soften the surface ever so slightly and allow the cloth to polish and shine it up. The white spirit meanwhile serves to remove any wax, dirt or fingermarks and the linseed oil helps to darken and camouflage any scratches and seal and tone down any areas where the finish has been removed (see Fig 5.9).

OTHER REVIVERS

The basic formula described above can be adapted to suit the needs of your project, such as increasing the amount of white spirit in the formula to combat an excessive presence of wax on the surface.

Polyurethane and other modern finishes can be revived by cleaning the surface with white spirit, with a little car rubbing compound stirred in, and then wiping some Danish oil (see page 100) on any areas which have bare wood exposed by scratches or deterioration.

Wax or oil finishes can be revived with a mixture of equal quantities of white spirit and water, stroked on to the surface with a clean cloth. Follow this process with a fresh application of oil or wax.

Fig 5.9 The before and after effects of the application of a reviver.

CHIPS IN THE FINISH

Very thick finishes can be chipped, leaving crater-like formations. These can be repaired by replacing the missing finish.

First establish the type of finish. This done, if any colour has been added to the finish you will have to try and match it by mixing in a comparable stain (see Chapter 12). Polyurethane finishes should be coloured with oil stains, French polish or cellulose finishes should be coloured with spirit stains.

Process:

1 Clean out the crater with a brush dipped in white spirit and allow to dry.
2 Fill the crater with the correct finish by dropping it in on the end of a stick or artist's brush, and try to overfill it.
3 Repeat (2) as necessary to achieve the desired overfilled effect.
4 Allow to dry for at least three days. If the chip is on a corner, you may need to turn the furniture over so that the new finish does not run out of the crater. If necessary, surround the crater with a clay or plasticine wall to keep the finish in while it dries (see Fig 5.10).

5 Level the surface with wet-or-dry paper followed by a fine rubbing compound until the surface is absolutely smooth.

Cellulose and other modern finishes can be repaired in this way using clear nail polish.

GARDEN FURNITURE

Garden furniture is often finished with linseed oil or some other preparation that in time becomes discoloured. On older furniture there may also be grime and algae. All of these can be removed using stripper and a wire suede brush, as described in Chapter 7. When stripped, refinish with Danish oil (see page 100).

Fig 5.10 Chips in thick finishes, such as modern lacquers, can be repaired by building a clay or plasticine wall around the damaged area and pouring the appropriate finish into it. Once the finish has hardened (with lacquers this can take anything up to seven days), the wall is removed and the area rubbed down with fine grade wet-and-dry before being polished with rubbing compound.

6
REPAIRING VENEERS

Veneers are sheets of wood, which can be as thick as the cover of a hardback book or as thin as a sheet of newspaper. They have been used in the decoration of every class of furniture for thousands of years, and have two primary uses: decorative and practical.

DECORATIVE

As decoration, veneers can be employed as marquetry (composing 'veneer pictures') or as a decorative device on the surface of furniture.

PRACTICAL

Many timbers are unsuitable for use in making solid wood furniture, perhaps because of the wildness of the grain, or because the structure of the wood is not solid enough to achieve the required solidity and strength. Alternatively, the wood may be too rare or too expensive to make such solid wood construction viable or environmentally friendly.

In such cases furniture is constructed from a cheap and stable foundation wood and then covered with a more attractive veneer.

In 1863 an American system was developed using veneers glued on top of one another to produce large strong sections of board called plywood (see Fig 6.1). This has the great advantage of being available in large sections and will not move,

Fig 6.1 Here you can see how plywood is constructed from sheets of thin veneers.

Fig 6.2 Chipboard covered with a very thin veneer.

expand, contract or split as solid wood does, and manufacturers soon developed designs which took advantage of these qualities.

Much early twentieth-century furniture is made in this way and is usually very robust and resilient. More modern furniture sometimes incorporates veneers glued to chipboard or blockboard, and these veneers can be extremely thin on some pieces (see Fig 6.2).

IDENTIFYING VENEERS

Being able to spot a veneer is important, as they require a rather different treatment from the restorer's point of view. Because they are so thin they must not be sanded or scraped with any degree of vigour, or exposed to too much water which could soften the glues, create bubbles or cause the base wood to swell up.

Spotting decorative veneers is relatively easy; they speak for themselves as being obviously marquetry. Practical veneers are a little more difficult to identify. Begin by looking at the edges of the table top or other area suspected of being veneered plywood. The sides will not have any end grain, and the edges may be concealed with an edging veneer – a thin strip of top veneer applied along the edge of the board. Occasionally veneered boards are 'lipped' with solid wood, and just as often the edges are camouflaged with brown paint, which comes off when (or if) the piece is stripped.

The side and back panels of cabinet furniture are often made of veneered plywood. The wood in these areas may be of a different type or grain structure to the outer and more visible parts, and this will be an indication of veneered plywood.

DAMAGED VENEERS

Identification of a veneered surface becomes much easier if it is damaged, and some forms of damage are unique to veneers. The two most common forms of damage are:

▮ Veneers becoming unstuck at the edges, snagging on something (such as a polishing cloth), breaking off and becoming lost (see Fig 6.3).

▮ Veneers becoming raised or 'bubbled' (see Fig 6.4).

Fig 6.3 Veneers frequently break off and become lost, as shown here.

Fig 6.4 Raised veneer.

LOST VENEERS

The easiest way to cure a missing piece of veneer is to fill the gap or crater with a suitable filler and then colour the filler to match the rest of the piece. Refer to Chapters 11 and 12 for more information on the type of filler and colour for your particular project (see Fig 6.5).

An alternative, particularly suited to replacing a large section of veneer, is to fill the gap with a new piece of veneer. A suitable piece of veneer is best obtained from a specialist supplier; advise them of your needs, and follow their advice – they are the most qualified and experienced people to help you in this respect. This done, use the following method:

1 Cut the veneer to shape. If the missing piece was an irregular shape, first scrape out any glue or other debris from the bottom of the crater with a suitable knife or chisel, then clean it out with an old toothbrush and white spirit.

2 Place a thin piece of paper over the crater and rub some pencil graphite over your index finger. Rub the crater through the paper, concentrating on the edges of the depression, and an exact likeness of the recess will be created on the paper, which you can use as a guide to cut out the replacement piece.

3 Take care to choose the best grain configuration you can, and then use a craft knife with a new

Fig 6.5 A good example of broken veneer which will need to be filled and then coloured to match the rest of the piece. The damage to this veneered box is due to the solid wood warping, and breaking the veneer as a result.

blade to cut out the shape. Coarse-grained veneers can be tricky to cut and prone to splitting; overcome this by gluing some of the veneer glue film on to the back before you begin to cut (see 'Glue film' in Chapter 2, page 15).

4 Now glue the replacement veneer into place by rubbing the tip of a medium-hot iron over the section, protecting the surface of the veneer with a damp cloth. Try not to warm up the surrounding veneers as this may soften *their* glue and give you even more work to do.

The same process applies to broken areas of sheet veneer: cut a clean edge around the break and fill it with a new veneer in the same way (see Fig 6.6).

RAISED OR BUBBLED VENEERS

Bubbles tend to be more prevalent in pre-war pieces, perhaps due to the glue manufacturing process or simply because they are older. Bubbles occur for three reasons:

▮ Heat or damp can penetrate the veneer, dissolving the animal glue and causing the veneer to swell up, lift and create a bubble.

▮ During manufacture the craftsperson may have missed a small section of gluing; once this area is subject to damp the veneer quickly expands and lifts.

▮ The glue may have been allowed to cool and dry before the veneer was laid on top.

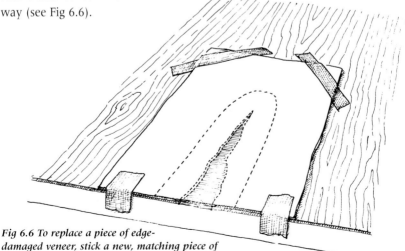

Fig 6.6 To replace a piece of edge-damaged veneer, stick a new, matching piece of veneer over the damaged area, and then cut through both the new and the old veneer with a sharp knife. The new piece will then fit the old exactly.

Identifying *which* of the above is the cause is a matter of trial and error. Try the following approaches, all of which are based on the assumption that the glue used for laying older veneers was animal glue (traditional scotch glue – see page 14), which can be redissolved by the application of heat.

USING AN IRON

1 Put your iron on a medium setting and lay a piece of paper over the bubble to aid the slip of the iron and protect the wood. If the bubble is severe and feels brittle, run a little water over it to soften it during heating, and prevent it drying out causing shrinkage and resultant splitting.

2 Place the tip of the iron on the paper and move it around, pushing the bubble flat. Keep this up for two or three minutes until you feel the heat has penetrated the veneer and redissolved the glue you hope to be present underneath.

3 Even if glue is present, once the iron is removed the veneer can tend to lift again before the glue has time to set and stick. To overcome this, place a flat block of wood or a second, cold, iron over the repair, and press down hard until the area has cooled (another two or three minutes).

4 Veneers can sometimes stick temporarily under the forces of heat and pressure: to check this, tap it with your fingernail – a hollow sound indicates the glue hasn't set and more goes with the iron are required.

CUTTING INTO THE BUBBLE

If the above method fails, then the cause of the bubble is a lack of glue during manufacture. Cut into the base of the bubble with a sharp craft knife and insert a thin layer of PVA wood glue. I use an artist's palette knife for this job, although a thick feeler gauge would work equally well. Once the glue is spread, squeeze the veneer down to remove excess glue and then clamp the bubble down as shown in Fig 6.7. Clamping in this way needs two pairs of hands and some preparation, so be sure to do a dry run beforehand.

REMOVING AND REPLACING

If a bubble has already broken open then you must assume that over the years a small but significant quantity of dust, dirt and wax will have collected in the resulting pocket. This will make it impossible for any remaining glue to stick the veneer back. If a previous restorer has tried to fix the problem and failed, there

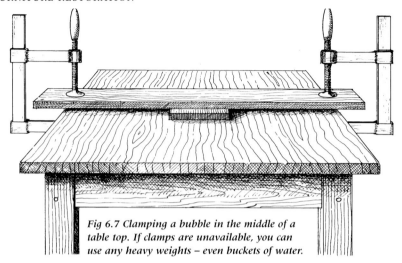

Fig 6.7 Clamping a bubble in the middle of a table top. If clamps are unavailable, you can use any heavy weights – even buckets of water.

may also be a quantity of glue present from this failed attempt, making things even more difficult for you. The veneer must be removed from over the bubble and the dirt, glue, wax and other accumulated substances cleaned out.

To do this, force the veneer open using an old kitchen knife, and then lift it off the top. Keep your hand cupped over the bubble because small brittle pieces of veneer can sometimes fly across the room, necessitating a time-wasting search among the shavings.

It is better to break the veneer away rather than cut it away with a sharp knife, because when you eventually have to stick the pieces of veneer back they will make a more natural join.

Once the veneer has been removed, scrape away the old deposits with a small knife or thin chisel and then wash the area

thoroughly with a toothbrush loaded with white spirit to remove any wax or dirt. Do the same to the back of the veneer and then allow to dry. Be meticulous in your preparation and you will be rewarded. Once you have thoroughly cleaned and dried all the surfaces, iron the veneer into place as before.

IF ALL ELSE FAILS

If you find the job you have done looks awful, you can always replace your repaired veneer with some filler, as described on page 35, and use an artist's brush and some spirit stains to 'paint' a veneer effect. On some woods this can be both an easy and very effective solution.

If even this approach fails, consider the 'life-saver' finishes: ebonizing (see Chapter 17) and painting (see Chapter 18).

7
STRIPPING

If the condition of a piece is such that repair is impracticable, stripping may be the answer. By stripping off the old finish you will remove decades of scratches, marks, water stains and other evidence of a long and battered life. Often, all you will need to do is replace it with a new finish and the furniture is as good as new, if not better – ready for another two or three generations of use.

CONSIDERATIONS BEFORE STRIPPING

If your project is an antique, take great care before deciding to strip; this may be ruinous as it will remove the piece's 'character' as well as more serious marks and blemishes, and loss of character means loss of value. Such pieces may be better served by reference to Chapter 8, which describes a sympathetic approach to repairing and refinishing antiques.

If the piece has a wax finish, this too may benefit from rejuvenation rather than stripping; Chapter 13 provides more information.

Before stripping any piece it is worth trying out some of the repairing techniques described in the last two chapters, if only because it will give you experience of the techniques without having to worry about the outcome as you will be stripping the piece in any case.

This chapter presumes that your furniture is of little value and can only be improved by stripping and refinishing.

CHEMICAL STRIPPER

For the majority of projects I would recommend paint/varnish stripper (see Fig 7.1). Do not be misled by its name – it will strip most finishes. Use this unless you have a very good reason for using one of the alternatives (see page 44).

Stripper is a caustic chemical compound which softens most types of wood finish, thus allowing the finish to be easily scraped off the wood. Always opt for a *thick* gel – avoid the thinner types which are available. Both types do the same job but the thicker stuff drips less and is therefore a bit easier to use. Once the bulk of the finish is removed, any remaining stripper is washed off the wood and neutralized using white spirit or methylated spirit depending on the type of stripper you buy.

Fig 7.1 Various makes of chemical stripper along with a bottle of methylated spirits, used to neutralize the stripper after application.

I advise against water-washable stripper; water raises the grain of the wood and lifts veneers as well as having an adverse effect on subsequent finishes. Stick with a spirit-washable stripper, and buy the appropriate spirit at the same time; a recommendation usually appears on the back of the stripper container.

SAFETY

When stripping make sure:

▍ No children or pets are present.
▍ You are working in a well-ventilated area.
▍ You wear gloves to prevent skin irritation (stripper causes mild burning to the skin), and have a bowl of water handy to wash off accidental splashes.
▍ You wear goggles to protect your eyes.

USING CHEMICAL STRIPPER

1   Place the item to be stripped on a carpet of old newspaper to protect the floor, preferably raised so that it is at a comfortable working height.
2   Pour some stripper into a wide-necked jar.
3   Apply the stripper using an old paint brush of a suitable size (3in or 76mm for large pieces, 1in or 25mm for small).
4   Strip small sections at a time, *not all at once*. Hence, apply stripper to one leg, allow to work, then strip the leg, making sure that that section is completely finished, before moving on the the next leg, and so on.

The type of tool you use to strip the finish depends on the area and shape of the wood. A paint scraper can be used in many cases, but larger flat areas are best stripped with a wallpaper scraper. Small flat areas are easily stripped using a chisel or a knife, but if the article is carved or the surface is not flat then you will need to use tools such as lollipop or similar small sticks shaped with a craft knife to get into the nooks and crannies successfully (see Fig 7.2). Curved surfaces can also be stripped using wire wool.

Gently scrape away the gunge that is a combination of the stripper and the chemically dissolved finish. Only proceed with stripping if the finish comes away easily; if it resists, leave the stripper to react for a further few minutes before trying again (see Fig 7.3).

Fig 7.2 Using a shaped stick to strip awkward areas of a turned leg.

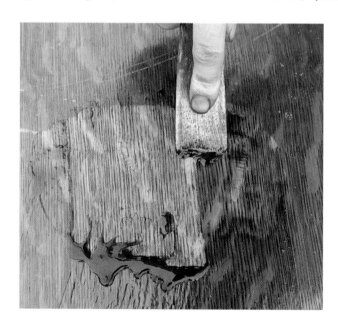

Fig 7.3 Scrape away the gunge after the stripper has softened the finish, depositing it in a soft cloth as you go along.

FINISHING OFF

If, after cleaning all the gunge off, there are still some remnants of finish left, repeat the process until all the finish is removed and you are left with bare wood and some residual gunge. This is removed by dipping some medium-grade wire wool in some white spirit or meths, and rubbing gently over the wood with a cleaning action (see Fig 7.4). Leave to dry and you have finished. Now repeat the process on the rest of the article, but remember, small sections at a time. If you use white spirit to clean off and neutralize the stripper you may find the surface of the wood is coated with a white powdery deposit. This is normal and should be ignored (see Fig 7.5).

I have already described some of the tools that can be used for scraping away gunge. However, the best tip I can give you is to buy a suede brush, as mentioned in Chapter 2. They are just the correct stiffness to scrape away the chemical gunge from carved and intricate areas and are particularly effective on very open grained woods such as oak, ash, elm and mahogany. These are all common hardwoods, widely used in all sorts of woodwork.

When such woods have been used in older furniture, they will often have been finished with a dark brown French polish which fills the open grain. The only way to strip these woods effectively is to remove the finish as described and then give the surface of the wood one more thin coating of stripper and scrub the pores of the open-grained wood with the suede brush.

Fig 7.4 Once you have removed the gunge, rub the area with wire wool dipped in white spirit or meths. This will remove any remaining gunge and stripper in preparation for refinishing.

*Fig 7.5
A harmless white
powdery residue
often remains
when white spirit
is used to clean off
stripper, as you
can see here.*

This will clean the old finish out completely, revealing the previously obscured wood (see Fig 7.6).

Once you have been through the stripping process a couple of times you will gain confidence and be able to strip a small table or uncomplicated chair in about an hour. If you have anything larger to strip, take it easy; don't try to do it all in one go – plan your work and spread it out over a number of sessions. Over-enthusiasm can be disastrous; good stripping takes time and it is important to do it properly to avoid disappointment.

Sometimes you will find it is only part of the furniture which

*Fig 7.6 A suede
brush is
indispensable
when stripping
carved and
complicated areas.*

needs stripping. Table tops for example, receive a lot of wear compared to the legs, and you may think it advisable to strip and refinish the top and leave the legs alone. However, this could give rise to colour matching problems, and if you are a relative beginner it is usually better in the long run to strip and refinish the whole piece.

STRIPPING UPHOLSTERED FURNITURE

When refinishing furniture in need of re-upholstery, first remove all the old upholstery, then strip, fix and refinish the woodwork before proceeding with the re-upholstery. If the upholstery is sound, you can refinish the woodwork without removing it as long as you are careful to protect the edges of the material with thick polythene and masking tape.

STRIPPING EMULSION PAINTED FURNITURE

Emulsion paint, as I have mentioned, has to be scraped, or sanded, off. Sometimes even these methods are not satisfactory, in which case I recommend you 'go with the flow': apply a fresh paint finish over the top and be done with it (see Chapter 18).

STRIPPING CELLULOSE LACQUERS

More modern post-war furniture will frequently be finished with cellulose lacquers, identified by the hard, clear, shiny finish and the fact that they often do not respond to ordinary paint stripper. Cellulose paint stripper is the answer. If this fails the finish is probably very recent indeed; try a hot air gun to soften it before scraping and lifting it away.

OTHER METHODS FOR STRIPPING

SANDING

I would only recommend this method when chemical stripper will not work (on modern finishes and emulsion paint for example), or when the finish comes off with great ease when sanded with a medium grade paper. This is often the case with old and deteriorated French polished surfaces, but the drawback is that the sanding will often remove a small quantity of wood and 'character' along with the finish, causing an uneven colour. Sanding is of course very labour intensive, and will require you to wear a mask to protect against the dust (see Chapter 3).

If sanding by hand, obtain a selection of sandpaper grades (see page 12), and, starting with the coarsest, begin to rub the finish off the wood. As it is slowly removed, move through the grades of paper, ending with the finest grade on the bare, smooth wood.

POWER TOOLS

I don't recommend these either because they are far too severe and can cause a lot of damage. If you do use a power tool you will still have to hand-strip mouldings and awkward areas with chemical stripper.

SCRAPING

Like sanding, this is a labour intensive procedure, and will also remove some wood along with the finish. I have never tried this method for major large-scale projects, but some restorers do find it very satisfactory, perhaps due to the avoidance of possible skin burns and the absence of chemical fumes, not to mention the fact it is extremely cheap!

Scrapers can take the form of chisels, knives, customized pieces of metal, broken hacksaw blades and broken glass. The most orthodox is the cabinet scraper, being specifically designed to scrape wood, and these can be obtained from any tool merchant. The tool consists of a piece of tool steel, sharpened along one edge. A certain amount of skill is required in use, but with practice the scraper can achieve a very fine surface.

BLOWTORCH

This tool is designed specifically to remove paint and other finishes and can be bought from DIY stores complete with a can of flammable gas.

This method removes thick layers of finish very quickly and is therefore most usefully employed when stripping large accumulations of household paint from window frames, doors and staircases. The heat causes the finish to soften, allowing it to be easily scraped away with a paint scraper. This operation is carried out with the torch in one hand and the scraper in the other and takes some practice to avoid charring the wood beneath. It clearly also requires care to prevent any danger of burning yourself. Wear a thick, non-flammable glove, and keep other finishes and chemicals well away from the flame. Be extra careful when working in daylight, as the flame becomes almost invisible in these conditions. As the smoke from some finishes can be toxic, be sure to have adequate ventilation, and always have a bowl of water to hand for skin burns or in case something catches fire.

It is unwise to try and strip furniture by this method unless it is of very simple design, or you intend to paint or ebonize the wood, thereby covering the inevitable charring.

HOT AIR GUN

A more recent development of the blowtorch is the hot air gun, which does not have a naked flame but works on a similar principle to a hairdryer, only much hotter (see Fig 7.7). It is a lot easier to control than a blowtorch and is less likely to cause charring and fire, while still having a similar softening effect on the finish.

Fig 7.7 A hot air gun.

SODA CRYSTALS

From my own hard-earned experience I offer you a word of advice: don't attempt to use soda crystals to strip a piece of furniture. It is tedious, time consuming and hazardous to your skin and anything else that gets splashed. More importantly they have an appalling effect on the wood, which, as part of the process, is soaked with water and is changed in colour to a dull grey.

DIPPING

This involves immersing the article in a large vat of chemicals for a period of time. The benefit is that it involves no work whatsoever: the job is usually undertaken by small firms and sometimes by second-hand shops who advertise the service in the local papers.

The success of such a process depends largely on the type of item to be dipped. I have yet to see a piece of furniture which has been dipped which could not have been stripped more effectively by hand using chemical stripper. Doors and larger architectural pieces are the kinds of items which are usually subjected to dipping, and I do not recommend it to furniture restorers as it can cause serious damage.

If you are interested in this form of stripping, contact a local specialist firm and ask about the possible results, at the same time asking to see an example of furniture they have stripped. Do not dip items of any value or anything with a veneered surface (see Chapter 6).

8
ANTIQUE FURNITURE AND ANTIQUIKSTRIP

The eleventh commandment of anyone with a knowledge of antiques is: do not strip antique furniture. This is very good advice, particularly for the absolute beginner. If the furniture is of any value, leave it alone, at least until you have had a chance to build up some experience and confidence with costly pieces.

If you strip a piece of antique furniture you will remove much of its 'character' or 'patina', and, as I have said, for many enthusiasts of old and antique furniture the patina is the proof of a piece's age and one of the reasons for buying it. A connoisseur can see the age of a piece of furniture through the depth and colour of its surface. Often, when stripping a piece of furniture, we remove many of the signs of its age and if it is a collectable antique, stripping will always be detrimental to its value.

Of course, what is and what is not antique will depend on your definition of the term. I like to define items made before 1920 as antique. There are many fine examples of furniture of this age around that are of little monetary value; in fact much 'antique' furniture is inexpensive if not virtually worthless, and valued for its function as opposed to its rarity or collectability. However, just because it is not expensive does not mean that we should not appreciate its patina, character and charm, and treat it with sympathetic techniques which will preserve these attributes. Antiquikstrip is one such technique.

HOW TO DO IT

This technique is for use on old French-polished furniture in need of stripping. Before trying it I would recommend you read Chapter 15, in order to first achieve a reasonable level of confidence and familiarity with the French polishing process.

Antiquikstrip removes just some of the blemished French polish finish, leaving the wood (which contains elements of the patina) and the underlying polish undisturbed.

If you have large gouges or scratches to repair, fill them with thick French polish as described on page 77 before using the antiquikstrip method.

1 Dip some medium-grade wire wool in some methylated spirit and squeeze away the excess.

2 Stroke small areas of the old finish, working with the grain, and around the furniture systematically. The top layers of the old polish will soon be removed by the action of the wire wool (see Fig 8.1).

3 Change the wire wool as soon as it becomes too clogged.

As methylated spirit is highly flammable, do not smoke or carry out the antiquikstrip process near an open flame.

The idea is to remove the part of the French polish which contains the scratches and deteriorated polish, and any other offensive aberrations, leaving a surface free of blemishes. With practice this can be achieved quickly just by removing the very top layer. The amount of finish to be removed is something you have to judge for yourself with each individual project.

4 Once the top layers have been removed, allow the remaining polish to dry out for a few hours and then rub down with 600 grit

Fig 8.1 Antiquikstrip in action. By rubbing gently over the top of the old French polish with some meths and wire wool, you can clean and partially strip the finish.

wet-or-dry paper to flatten the surface for the next stage.

5 Now French polish the surface as directed in Chapter 15. You do of course have a head start in that the foundation of the polish is already in place.

6 Continue to build up the polish, and spirit off or wire wool a satin finish depending on your preference.

Given the right conditions and experience, this technique is extremely flexible in that you can choose which scratches to leave and which to remove or reduce in visual impact. However, you should be aware that the technique works best on relatively thick polish which has been damaged by scratching and other marks. Sometimes the French polish will be too deteriorated to provide a foundation.

If you have a piece of French-polished furniture beyond hope of salvation which has been earmarked for chemical stripping, try antiquikstrip on it first to gain some experience.

9
REPAIRING STRUCTURAL DAMAGE

Whereas the surface ailments described in Chapter 5 were superficial, there are structural problems which can totally disable a piece of furniture. Such damage frequently leads to pieces being consigned to the rubbish dump.

To the furniture restorer, pieces like this are a double-edged sword. On the one hand, such problems are tricky and time consuming to put right, whereas on the other, such pieces can be picked up for next to nothing, if not free from a skip or a rubbish dump.

Fixing such furniture requires tools, equipment and possibly some woodwork, but it is some of the most satisfying to restore. However, do beware of furniture with parts actually missing; as I said earlier, such pieces can prove very expensive and fall out of the scope of this book.

WOBBLY CHAIRS

Wobbliness is the most common symptom of structural damage to be found in furniture, and the advice that is given here for chairs can easily be applied to any wobbly or loose pieces.

Wobbliness is usually caused by the glued joints which hold the furniture together failing. Central

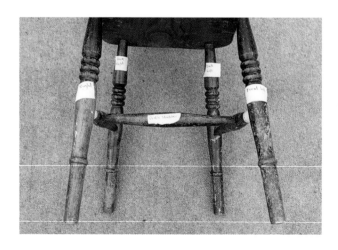

Fig 9.1 Remember to label each component part of a piece before you dismantle it.

heating has increased the prevalence of this problem, by drying out and shrinking wood joints.

DISMANTLING A CHAIR

The solution is to dismantle the chair and separate all the weak joints. It is wise to try and reglue all the joints, even if one or two remain difficult to separate. Thus, before dismantling, describe and label the position of each component part. The labels should describe exactly what side and in which direction the part was facing (see Fig 9.1). More complicated pieces may require a sketch or photo, but *do do it*; even the simplest pieces can otherwise be nightmares to get back together again.

If joints do prove difficult to part, give them a thorough inspection to make sure you are pulling them in the right direction and there are no concealed dowels, screws or nails holding them together. If you still have problems, try the following:

▌ Use a mallet to apply force to the joint. Tape some protective cardboard or cloth pads to the areas where you intend the mallet to strike. Secure the piece in a vice with the jaws similarly lined, and start to gently tap the joint (see Fig 9.2).

Fig 9.2 Gently tap the joint with a mallet.

▌ If this fails, try a car scissor jack. Place this in the most appropriate position, pack any gaps with blocks of wood or old books and start winding the jack up (see Fig 9.3).

▌ If the jack fails, the joint will almost certainly remain secure for the next 100 years and is best left well alone.

Fig 9.3 If the joints prove stubborn, try forcing them apart using a car scissor jack.

Fig 9.4 Scrape the joints clean with a chisel.

CLEANING THE JOINTS

Once the piece is dismantled as far as you can realistically dismantle it, you need to clean the joints in preparation for regluing and reassembly.

Use an old chisel or other sharp edge to scrape off the old glue from around the wood that comprises the joints (see Fig 9.4). Protect your eyes for this job as old glues can be very brittle and are liable to fly in all directions.

To clean the holes, use a ¼in (6mm) chisel, and try to clean as much of the glue out as possible.

BROKEN JOINTS

If you find the wood comprising a joint or joints turns out to be broken you can either cut out the joint and 'let in' a new piece of wood, or rebuild the joint with car body filler. The first method will require the assistance of a cabinetmaker, so the second is well worth considering.

Method:

1 Clean the wood thoroughly with white spirit and a suede brush.
2 Drill some ⅛in (3mm) holes into the remaining wooden part of the joint so that the filler can get a good grip and bond successfully with the remaining part of the joint.
3 Reassemble the joint with car body filler as shown in Chapter 11.

If the furniture is assembled using dowels (see Fig 9.5) you may find some get broken when you take the piece apart. Most DIY stores sell dowel, and many sell ready made dowel pegs. Check the depth of the joints concerned by inserting a pencil into the holes.

*Fig 9.5
A dowelled joint
being cleaned up,
showing the
dowel pegs.*

Dowel broken off in the hole must be drilled out before being replaced. First cut the protruding dowel off at the base with a hacksaw so it is flush. Hold the

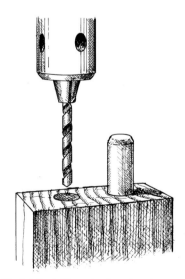

Fig 9.6 To drill out broken dowels, start with a small drill bit and drill in the centre of the dowel. You may find it easier if you cut the remaining dowel at the base.

wood in a vice and drill a $\frac{1}{8}$in (3mm) pilot hole dead centre of the embedded dowel (see Fig 9.6). Then drill a slightly bigger hole and continue this process until the hole is the same size as the dowel. If the drill goes off course or you make the hole too big you can fill the hole with filler and try again.

REASSEMBLY

This can, as I have indicated, be harder than it first appears. Success depends on labelling the pieces in advance, staying calm and not being disturbed. Then follow this process:

1 Do a dry run of assembling the piece without glue. This allows you to check all the pieces are there, all fit, and the labelling system works.
2 Go through what you have just done in your mind's eye a few

times so you know exactly what to do. If the project is large, remember to glue and reassemble the small parts first, then fit them all together into the whole.

3 Have a damp cloth ready to clean up excess glue.

4 Establish whether you need clamps during the dry run. If the construction can stand up by itself at this stage without falling apart, the joints are firm and don't open up, then you probably don't. If you do, adjust them to the correct opening and have some cardboard or wood protectors taped into place.

5 Make sure you have the right glue for the job (see Chapter 2).

6 Work methodically through the dry assembly stage, attending to one joint at a time.

7 Coat both members of the joint with glue, and be liberal; too much can always be cleaned off, too little can be a disaster.

8 Bond the members together, and move on swiftly to the next joint.

9 Once all the members have been glued, squeeze the joints together tightly and ensure the piece is sitting square.

10 If you are using clamps, apply them in two stages: first hold

Fig 9.7 The clamps in place and tightened up.

Fig 9.8 Here you can see the glue oozing from a joint after tightening. Clean away any such excess glue with a damp cloth.

them in the correct position, and tighten them just enough to hold their own weight. When they are all in place, slowly tighten them up one at a time (see Fig 9.7). Once tightened, check for squareness and clean off excess glue with a damp cloth (see Fig 9.8).

11 Check all four legs are touching level ground. You can simulate a level floor with a flat piece of thick plywood placed on your bench.

12 When you clean up the glue keep changing the cloth so that it does not redeposit glue on the furniture. Use knives and bits of stiff card to get close into the joints where most of the glue exudes.

13 Ten minutes after gluing check no joints have opened up, but *do not pull at them.*

14 Leave the piece to set overnight.

15 The following day, clean off any glue that has oozed out during the night with a sharp knife or chisel, and the job is done!

If the chair does not sit square on the floor after all, check the floor is level; they rarely are. Do this by rotating the chair by 90° and seeing if the same wobble occurs. If it does the floor is flat and the legs are at fault. If the wobble changes to another leg or disappears, it's the floor. Double check by repeating the test, rotating in the other direction.

If the legs are out of order you must true one of them up. To do this, buy a chair stud (from DIY shops all over the land) and apply it to the shortest leg. Alternatively cut and glue a suitably sized piece of wood to the bottom of the shortest leg. After the glue has dried you can stain and finish accordingly.

Whatever you do, do not saw bits off the legs; this way leads to madness.

REMOVING OLD SCREWS

Old screws are often corroded and very difficult to remove. If they don't come out easily first time, ask yourself if they really need to be removed. If they do, make sure you have the right tool for the job: a good-quality, correct-fitting screwdriver. Make sure the slot at the top of the screw is clean and not blocked. Remove any debris using an old chisel or knife, until the screwdriver sits perfectly in the slot.

Next, clamp the furniture firmly to the top of a bench so that the screw head is pointing skywards (or get someone to hold the piece for you as you work).

METHOD 1

Grip the screwdriver in both hands, bend your knees and turn your whole body at the waist. Do not try to twist your wrists or arms; they do not possess nearly as much strength as the rest of your body (see Fig 9.9).

First try to tighten the screw (always clockwise), which can help break some of the corrosion surrounding it. Then try to loosen it by twisting anticlockwise. As you turn, push downwards with all your weight to prevent the screwdriver jumping out of the screw slot.

METHOD 2

If this fails, protect the piece and the worksurface you are using with a thick blanket, locate the screwdriver

Fig 9.9 Use a correct-sized screwdriver and a firm grip to remove stubborn screws.

in the screw slot and strike the top of the tool with a mallet or lump of wood. The first blow should just tap the top of the screwdriver, the second should be a little harder, and the third should help loosen the screw. Do not overdo it and make sure the screwdriver has a shatterproof handle.

Now repeat Method 1.

METHOD 3

If even Method 2 and Method 1 combined still fail to budge the screw, and assuming you haven't changed your mind about removing it, heat a length of metal rod with the same dimensions as the top of the screw head to a dull red heat and touch it on to the screw. Leave it there until the heat has had enough time to conduct through the screw (remember to keep any flammable preparations well out of the way during the process).

Now repeat Method 1.

If Method 3 fails after a few attempts, give up. A more likely outcome however is that the screw will have broken, in which case you will have to call it a draw. When you remove the other screws you will find the remains of the screw in the wood, and will be able to remove it using pliers, or cut it back with a hacksaw.

Fig 9.10 Use a block to increase leverage and protect the wood.

REMOVING OLD NAILS AND PINS

Nails and pins should not be in furniture at all, but unfortunately they frequently are, particularly in wobbly chairs.

Try to remove nails using a pair of pliers or a claw hammer. If you need extra leverage, use a block under your chosen tool (see Fig 9.10). You will often have to resort to brute force and simply wrench the two pieces of wood apart and remove nails and pins afterwards. Any resulting splits or breaks in the timber will then also have to be repaired with filler.

WORN DRAWER RUNNERS

These are the bits of wood that drawers use to rest upon the corresponding bits of wood in the cabinet (see Fig 9.11). There are usually two parts to a drawer runner that need repair – the part inside the cabinet and the part attached to or inset into the drawer itself.

It is difficult to describe when drawer runners need replacing, but when a drawer starts to stick and will not sit level in its opening in the cabinet, take it out and inspect the insides of the cabinet and the bottom of the drawer sides for excessive wear.

There are a number of configurations of drawer runners, all

Fig 9.11 One example of a drawer runner configuration. The channel in the middle of the drawer side is matched by an insert in the body of the cabinet. These will often wear and, in extreme cases, need replacing.

of which are likely to require some woodworking skills and equipment. If you are not experienced in woodworking it would be wise to engage the services of a weekend cabinetmaker. Of course, there is no reason why you should not learn the skills required as time goes by; you will find them very useful in your furniture restoration, as the problem of worn drawer runners is very common.

REPAIRING BROKEN DRAWERS

Drawers often collapse due to overwork or misuse. In such cases you will need to scrape off the old glue and reassemble. If any of the components have broken or split you will need to glue, clamp and allow them to dry before gluing the drawer back together again.

NATURAL SPLITS IN THE WOOD

Where the wood has split along the grain, such breaks are caused by the wood drying out and shrinking. It usually splits along the grain starting from a section of end grain (see Fig 9.12), and the easiest remedy is to fill the crack and colour accordingly (see Chapter 11).

SPLITS IN TABLE TOPS

During the manufacture of table tops, two or more pieces of wood are often joined together to form a larger or more stable piece of wood. Over the years, the constant fluctuations in moisture from summer to winter can move apart, twist and warp these joints (see Fig 9.12). The problem is often exacerbated when small tables are

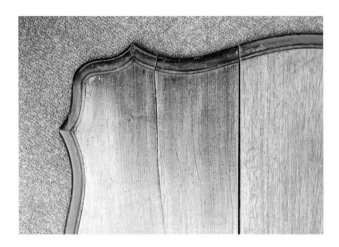

Fig 9.12 Two splits or breaks in a table top. The split on the right was caused by the wood shrinking and consequently breaking the joint between the two boards that make up the table top. The split on the left was caused by a defect in the timber itself.

used out of doors in summer and are caught in sudden summer storms. This has the dual effect of first drying out the wood and then saturating it.

To repair such damage:

1 If a split is only halfway up the join or less, remove the table top and break the join. (Many splits are such that the wood is already in one, two, three or even four pieces already.)
2 Allow the wood to dry.
3 Plane the edges of the boards that make up the table top so that they are true.
4 Glue them back together in the same manner as when the table was first made.

Once again, this process involves some woodworking skill and equipment. You may prefer to engage the services of your weekend cabinetmaker and get him or her to do the planing before you do the gluing.

You could also consider repairing less serious partial splits by filling and colouring (see Chapter 11).

WARPED TABLE TOPS

These often come in tandem with splits in table tops. The warping and twisting of table tops and cabinet tops cannot easily be repaired (see Fig 9.13). The force exerted by a twisting piece of wood is phenomenal, and extremely hard to control or repair.

The best remedy is to remove the table or cabinet top and replace it with a new one, either a copy of the original or a top made from thick plywood, and finish accordingly.

Fig 9.13 This beech table top became bowed after being left outside in the rain.

REPAIRING COMPLETE BREAKS IN FURNITURE

You will often come across a slat in a chair or other piece of furniture that is broken in two. To dismantle the piece, fix the break and reassemble would be unfeasible; far better to fix the slat *in situ*. This is the method.

1   Make sure the two pieces of wood are thoroughly clean.
2   Do a dry run, ensuring there are no foreign bodies or splinters preventing a good union between the two pieces. At the same time establish what method you will use to hold the pieces together while they dry. This could be any number of things: bulldog clips, masking tape, small clamps; it all depends on the nature of the job.

Experiment at the dry run stage to find the best solution.
3   Spread the glue, join, clamp and allow to dry (see Fig 9.14).

WOODWORM

Although woodworm (also known as the common furniture beetle) can do irreparable damage, as long as you know what to look for so that you can nip the problem in the bud, you have little to fear. Woodworm damage is often superficial, and typified by a smattering of tiny flight holes. Woodworm tend to prefer the rougher wood found at the back and underneath furniture, so always pull pieces away from the wall and inspect these areas thoroughly, looking out for any fine-powdered sawdust which is another indication of infestation.

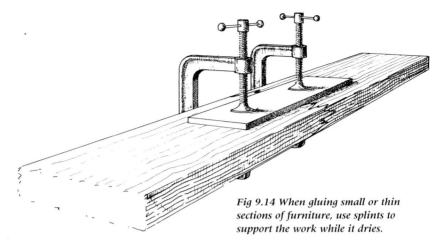

Fig 9.14 When gluing small or thin sections of furniture, use splints to support the work while it dries.

TREATING A LIGHT INFESTATION

Treatment of a light infestation is simple. Buy some woodworm-killing fluid from a DIY shop, and squirt it liberally into the flight holes. This will eradicate any insects still at home and stop woodworm fly from returning to lay more eggs. Always remember the fluid is a poison, and treat it accordingly.

TREATING A MORE SERIOUS INFESTATION

If you find an infestation late in the day, and parts of the structure have been undermined, there are two possible approaches:

Drill some ¼in (6mm) diameter holes through the deteriorated wood into solid wood underneath. Then fill the drill holes with fibreglass resin and allow it to soak into the deteriorated timber.

Fibreglass resin is available from car accessory shops, and when mixed according to the instructions will solidify and stabilize the wood. Any remaining holes can be filled with filler. Once the structure is firm again you can colour as necessary (see Chapter 12).

Alternatively, cut out the deteriorated wood and replace with some new wood of the same size, shape and type. For this you will need either some woodworking skills or the help of a weekend cabinetmaker.

REPAIRING CHIPBOARD

Fibreglass resin can also be used to repair chipboard. Chipboard is made by mixing small fibres or chips of wood in a glue and then compressing. It has hundreds of uses in modern furniture design, but when it breaks it is very difficult to repair. You should find the following method makes things easier.

1 Place the two broken sections together and clean out any chips that are obstructing the close union of the two sections.
2 Using plasticine or clay, make a wall around the break.
3 On the underside, seal the break with 2in (51mm) packaging tape so that no resin can seep out, and support the two sections by placing blobs of plasticine beneath the two halves on the corners, keeping the two sides on the same level.
4 Pour the fibreglass resin into the break and allow it to set. The chipboard will absorb the resin which, once set, will make a perfect bond.
5 Finish by filling any holes and colouring (see Chapters 11 and 12).

Finally, if chipboard has just had a piece removed or a corner damaged, it can be repaired by building up with car body filler (see Fig 9.15).

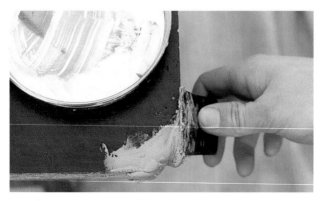

Fig 9.15 Building up a broken chipboard corner with car body filler.

10
FIXING ODDS AND ENDS

This chapter covers those elements of furniture restoration which do not fit neatly into the scope of subjects covered in Chapters 5 and 9. There follows a selection of common problems which are hard to pigeon-hole but which arise frequently.

KNOBS AND FINIALS

Knobs and finials (small decorative knobs) are often missing or in need of replacement. They can be bought from DIY stores, and for more individual needs there are firms who specialize in this kind of product. Also, dealers often retain these parts of otherwise useless furniture, so it is worth asking around in second-hand shops and junk shops if you are looking for a very specific replacement knob.

Decorative finials are very often lost or broken, and if you can't find a satisfactory replacement, you can cast one yourself.

CASTING A FINIAL

1   Lightly wax a matching finial and make an impression of it in plasticine (see Fig 10.1).
2   Mix some car body filler and spoon it into the mould (see Fig 10.2).
3   Cast the other half of the finial in the same way, but before it has set, push the two halves gently together, matching the complete finial (see Fig 10.3).
4   Clean up the rough edges, fill any air holes, stain, finish and replace!

LEATHER TOPS

Replacing a leather top is not difficult. The problem lies in ordering the correct size of leather. Most suppliers will require the exact measurement in millimetres (length and width), and if the piece you need is not square you will need to make a paper template of the recess into which it is to be fitted. The supplier will also need to know the colour and the type of decoration. You should find such specialists helpful and useful sources of information.

Old leather removed (it should come off extremely easily) and new leather successfully purchased, you

MAKING A FINIAL

Fig 10.1 Make an impression of a matching finial in plasticine.

Fig 10.2 Push some body filler into the impression.

Fig 10.3 Then repeat to make the other half. Before this is dry, push the two halves together to make a complete finial. Once the finial is finished, fill any air bubbles, tidy up the rough edges, stain with a spirit stain and French polish to the desired colour.

need to make sure that the recess is perfectly clean and flat. Be very fussy around the edge. To check for flatness, lay some thin paper where the leather is to be placed and run your hand over the top to see if any foreign bodies mark or raise the paper. Once the surface is clean and flat you can proceed to lay the new leather.

1 Brush some thick wallpaper paste on the area to be leathered and then check there are no lumps or dry spots.

2 Lay the leather on the surface and smooth from the centre outwards, removing any creases and air bubbles. Beware of stretching the leather at this stage.

3 Line up any decorative tooling so that it is parallel with the edges.

4 Using the back of a dinner knife, gently push the edges of the leather into the recess. Then, using a craft knife fitted with a new blade, cut around the line made by the dinner knife. If you have a metal ruler or straight edge, use this to guide the craft knife and hold the leather in place as you cut. Lean the craft knife outwards slightly from the centre of the leather so that it undercuts the edges (see Fig 10.4). This will help disguise the lighter-coloured edge of the leather.

5 When all sides have been cut, push the leather against the edge of the recess and clean up with a damp rag.

If you scuff or otherwise damage the leather during fitting it can be repaired using spirit stains (see Chapter 12). It's worth remembering that old leathers can sometimes be improved rather than replaced using the correct colour of

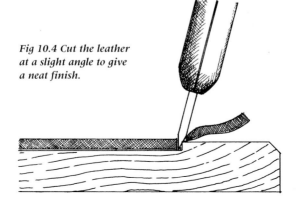

Fig 10.4 Cut the leather at a slight angle to give a neat finish.

spirit stain with a little French polish added. This can be rubbed on gently with a cotton cloth followed by a thin wax. How effective this proves will depend on the condition of the leather.

GLASS AND MIRRORS

Always handle glass and mirrors with extreme care, as glass is a very dangerous material as well as being expensive to replace.

If the frame does not need any structural repair it is best to leave the mirror in place while refinishing. Cover the workbench with a thick blanket and protect the glass using masking tape and paper (see Fig 10.5).

If you have to replace the glass itself, take the measurements to a glass merchant and have them cut it for you. Do *not* try to cut it yourself; this can be dangerous as it requires specialist knowledge and tools, as well as plenty of space.

If the glass itself is dirty, polish it with old newspaper dampened with methylated spirit. Any spots of paint can be removed with the edge of a sharp blade or alternatively a little metal polish.

Remember that glass used in cabinet doors is thin, so take great care when polishing and handling; never push down on it too hard.

GLUE BLOCKS

Old mirrors are often fixed into their frames by means of glue blocks (see Fig 10.6). If you do decide to remove the mirror before

Fig 10.5 When refinishing the frame of a mirror, shield the glass with tape and paper.

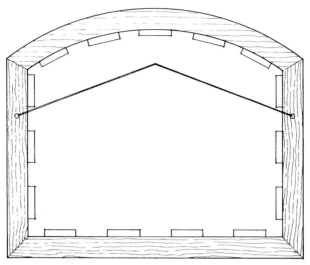

***Fig 10.6 The glue block used to be a common way of
constructing furniture. They are often to be found on the
reverse of old mirrors.***

refinishing the frame, the blocks can
be awkward to deal with as they are
often fixed with animal glue (see
Chapter 2). Such blocks are also
frequently seen underneath and
round the back of old cabinet
furniture (see Fig 10.7).

REMOVING GLUE BLOCKS

To remove glue blocks, lay some
cotton wool or cloth soaked in hot
water over the individual blocks and
wait for the glue to soften. If the
project has been stored in a damp
place or is very old, even this may
not be necessary; a sharp tap with a
light hammer on one end of the
block will suffice. Remember to
protect the backs of mirrors with

***Fig 10.7 Glue blocks are commonly found
on the inside of cabinet furniture.***

cardboard if you adopt this method, or, if this presents problems, lever the blocks off using a chisel.

REPLACING GLUE BLOCKS

This is more problematic. Assuming you do not want to attempt to fix the blocks with animal glue, you will have to find a way of holding each block in place while a modern, slower drying glue dries. There are several possible methods.

You can drill a hole in each block and screw them into place. This method is better suited to completely new blocks, which are easily made. Drill holes at 1in (25mm) intervals into some suitably sized quadrant moulding (available at all DIY stores). Then cut 1in (25mm) sections from the moulding, leaving the hole you have drilled in the middle of the block. Glue and screw these into place (see Fig 10.8).

The size of hole you drill depends on the width (gauge) of screw. The best way is to buy both items together and ask for advice on the best drill bit for your chosen screw size.

If you require large, strong glue blocks which will in any case be out of sight, you can buy plastic, pre-formed and pre-drilled fixing blocks. These do not require glue, just screws. Most DIY stores will have a

selection for you to choose from.

Finally, you can opt to use a heat-sensitive glue gun. Make sure you use a glue stick suitable for sticking wood, and that the old animal glue has been thoroughly cleaned off the wood if you are re-using the original blocks.

LOCKS

It is rare to find a lock with its original key on a cabinet, wardrobe or writing box, and hence the price of such an item with its original key can be up to twice as much as its keyless equivalent. In the same way that they keep undamaged knobs and finials from otherwise useless furniture, dealers also keep keys, and it is worth asking if you can try your local dealer's 'bunch'.

Failing this, you can send the lock to a cabinetmaker's locksmith who should be able to cut a key to fit. If there is no lock either, then the same suppliers can send you one by mail order.

The settings of locks are often damaged so that they are loose. This is easily remedied by filling around the lock recess with car bodywork filler and screwing the lock back into place. (Be careful not to clog up the mechanism of the lock with filler.) Once dry the filler can then be coloured as described in Chapter 12.

MAKING GLUE BLOCKS

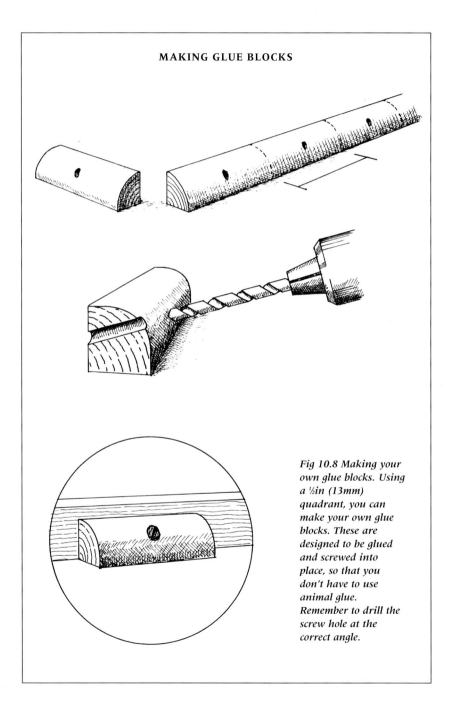

Fig 10.8 Making your own glue blocks. Using a ½in (13mm) quadrant, you can make your own glue blocks. These are designed to be glued and screwed into place, so that you don't have to use animal glue. Remember to drill the screw hole at the correct angle.

LOOSE SCREWS

The remedy for these is simple.

1 Remove the screw.
2 Push a matchstick or sticks dipped in glue into the hole.
3 Cut off any protruding matchstick with a sharp knife.
4 Replace the screw.

If the area around a hinge has split and the screw won't hold, fill with car body filler or urea-formaldehyde glue, and if necessary clamp the wood together until it is set.

METALS

CLEANING METALWORK

Metalwork can easily be cleaned with a rubbing compound or metal polish. Badly corroded, rusty or tarnished metal will need the application of a suede brush or fine wire wool.

RESTORING PLATED METALWORK

Sometimes, materials used in furniture can be plated. This means that one metal is coated with a very thin film of another metal, and inevitably, over the years, the outer coating can get worn away (see Fig 10.9). Remedies include:

- Replacing the metalwork altogether.
- Rubbing off the remaining plating with rubbing compound to reveal the lesser but at least homogenous base metal. (This can turn out surprisingly well on simple designs.)
- Painting the bare areas with gold or silver paint. This method is more suitable for decorative or complex designs.

Fig 10.9 An example of plated metal worn away.

11
FILLERS

'Filler' is a broad term used to describe a large number of compounds that can be applied to cracks, dents and other crevices found in furniture. Ideally, good application of the correct filler is the first step towards eradicating and making invisible damaged areas of your furniture – if you choose the right filler and take sufficient care, it is possible to carry out an invisible repair!

There are three different classes of filler which you need to be aware of: grain fillers, scratch fillers and wood fillers.

GRAIN FILLERS

These are used on open- or coarse-grained woods when a glossy or smooth final finish is required. The compound is rubbed into the bare wood so as to fill the texture and when dry is lightly sanded leaving the surface smooth and ready for a finish. Without the use of a grain filler the texture of a wood's grain will show through the finish and spoil the glossy smoothness. The application of French polish to a coarse-grained wood such as oak is a good example of the need for grain filling (see Chapter 15).

There are three methods of filling grain.

METHOD 1:
FINISH AS A FILLER

1   Brush your chosen finish on to the open-grained wood, allow it to dry and rub back with 600 grit wet-and-dry paper moistened with a little white spirit.
2   Repeat this process until the wood is as smooth as marble and the grain is filled with the finish.

In other words, this method uses the chosen finish as the filler. It takes a little longer than other filling methods but you are guaranteed a perfect colour match between the filler and the finish.

If you apply French polish as you refinish and you are a beginner, I suggest you apply the coats for this method using a rubber (see page 106), thereby practising your French-polishing skills, and as you grow more confident, move on to application using a brush (see page 119).

METHOD 2: PLASTER OF PARIS AS A FILLER

1 Prepare a bowl of plaster of Paris, and a bowl containing an equal mixture of water and methylated spirit.
2 Dip a ball of cotton cloth into the liquid mix and then dab it into the plaster.
3 Rub this into the grain of the wood, wiping off any wet slurry across the grain (see Fig 11.1). Try not to make the surface too wet as this will cause the grain to rise.
4 After about an hour the compound should be dry enough to be sanded with fine sandpaper followed by wet-and-dry paper.
5 The wood will now look less than desirable; a 'chalkboard effect' will have developed (see Fig 11.2). Take some boiled linseed oil and thin it with enough white spirit to give the oil a watery consistency.
6 Gently rub this into the wood and plaster using a clean rag. The filler will become invisible before your very eyes (see Fig 11.3). Clean off any excess oil, and allow to dry for 36 hours.
7 Now apply the finish of your choice.

Fig 11.1 Wet the cloth in the meths/water mix, dab it into the plaster of Paris, and rub into the pores of the wood.

Fig 11.2 The 'chalkboard' effect.

Fig 11.3 Here you can see the effect of applying the thinned linseed oil.
On the left hand side: before. On the right: after.

Often, when you are stripping old furniture you will find a white deposit in the grain. This is the plaster of Paris in which the oil has dried out. Just apply some more linseed oil, and the whiteness will disappear for another 100 years.

METHOD 3:
PROPRIETARY FILLER

Simply buy a pot of filler from your DIY shop and follow the instructions on the tin. Rub the compound into the grain, allow to dry, and sand off.

These compounds are closely related to clay and are available in a range of colours. Try to get as close a match as you can to the wood (see Fig 11.4). If this is not possible and the filler is conspicuous, then stain the grain filler to match the real wood before applying your chosen finish (see Fig 11.5).

Fig 11.4 Try to buy as closely colour-matched a filler as you can for the job.

Fig 11.5 If you cannot find the correct colour filler, all is not lost. A radically different colour can be used, such as here, and then stained to match the finish.

There are two types: fillers for scratches in the finish, and fillers for scratches in the wood.

The catch-all remedy for scratches in the finish is some form of wax. A suitable wax polish (see Chapter 13) will fill such scratches and is normally applied as part of regular cleaning and polishing.

Larger or deeper scratches can be treated with harder waxes or by pushing some coloured finishing wax into the scratches and allowing it to dry for 48 hours before buffing with a clean cloth.

WAX STICKS

These are intended for more severe cases and scratches which are visually offensive. They are sold variously as scratch removers, scratch covers and hole fillers and are available in a variety of colours from DIY stores.

I have reservations about wax sticks. First, they cost far in excess of the raw materials which make them up (wax and pigment). Second, although the manufacturers offer a wide range of colours, the number of colours in any one scratch can be two, three or even four (see Fig 11.6). A stick will only fill such scratches with one colour, which is sometimes woefully inadequate; the visually jarring scratch simply becomes a visually jarring streak of coloured wax!

BLENDING YOUR OWN WAX

The first drawback can be overcome by making your own sticks. Before mixing the colours for your sticks, refer to the colour wheel on page 94 which will help to explain basic

Fig 11.6 This scratch needs at least two colours to fill and camouflage it correctly. These children's crayons can be mixed with each other in order to match the colours of the wood.

colour mixing theory. Browns are best achieved by mixing two complementary colours: red and green, purple and yellow, orange and blue.

1 Obtain some children's wax crayons – the thick ones are best. You will also need an old tablespoon and a source of heat. I use the gas cooker but a blowtorch or candle will work just as well (see Fig 11.7).
2 Hold the tablespoon in a heat-proof cloth, and heat it over the flame; it will warm up very quickly.
3 Remove the spoon from the heat and touch the bottom of the hot spoon with, for example, an orange crayon. This will melt and become liquid.
4 Once you have enough wax in the bottom of the spoon, do the same with a blue crayon. Swill the first few drops of blue wax around, returning the spoon to the heat if necessary. As you do so the colours will mix and you will see the orange wax go a shade closer to brown. The more blue you add the more brown it will become. As the two or three colours needed to fill a scratch are usually shades of one colour, you can mix the lightest first, then add more and more blue to create the darker shades required.

Pour the molten wax directly into the scratch (see Fig 11.8). This is the best method, especially on larger gouges and blemishes as it has a better grip.

Fig 11.7 Melting and combining the colours to match the wood, using the spoon and blowtorch method.

Fig 11.8 Pouring the melted wax into the scratch while it is still hot.

You'll need to experiment to find the right colour for your particular piece of wood. Look intently at the colour of the wood and see if you can observe traces of yellow, green, red, or any other colour. If you can, add a little of that colour to your brew and evaluate its effect. Practice makes perfect, and don't forget to always view your work in natural light.

If your colour is not exactly right first time, scrape the wax from the scratch and have another go. Fig 11.9 (pages 78–9) shows the technique of pouring one colour wax into a scratch, then removing the area that needs to be darker and replacing it with that darker-toned colour, achieving an 'invisible mend'.

Once you have the correct colour match, remove any excess wax around the repair by rubbing gently with a cloth lightly dampened with white spirit and water.

FILLING SCRATCHES IN FRENCH POLISH

One way to fill such scratches is to clean up the bottom of the scratch with white spirit and a toothbrush, and drop in some thickened French polish, made by pouring some polish into a dish and allowing it to dry out. As the alcohol (meths) evaporates, the polish thickens. Take some of this on to a matchstick and touch it into the hole or scratch (see Fig 11.10 on page 80). Allow to harden, and repeat as necessary. Once the filler polish is completely dry, rub the protruding filler with wet-and-dry and then polish the area with some rubbing compound or other abrasive cream.

The same process can be applied to other types of hard finish such as polyurethane and cellulose, and can also be used to fill overlooked depressions in a newly French polished surface. On very deep scratches it may be worth using transparent French polish to avoid a darkening of the filled area with the layers of polish.

USING WAX TO REPAIR A SCRATCH

Fig 11.9(a) Fill the scratch with wax.

Fig 11.9(b) Scrape away any excess with a blade, and then rub away and smooth down the wax with white spirit and a cloth.

Fig 11.9(c) When smooth, use a sharp knife or pin to pick out the areas where a darker colour is required.

Fig 11.9(d) Fill these scratches with darker wax, and scrape and rub down with white spirit as before.

Fig 11.9(e) Any excess wax is removed with a cloth lightly dampened with white spirit and water.

Fig 11.10 If you intend to finish your project by French polishing it, then fill scratches with thick French polish, as shown.

WOOD FILLERS

There are two main types of filler that I suggest the beginner becomes familiar with: one is commonly called stopping, and the other is somewhat unconventional: car body filler.

STOPPING

This filler can be water, white spirit or cellulose based. All of these should have a smooth, clay-like texture, making the filler easy to push into small scratches and dents.

Stopping comes ready to use in small tins (see Fig 11.11). These can tend to allow the filler to dry out and go unworkably hard. If this happens you can usually resoften it by adding a compatible solvent.

A variety of 'woody' colours are available, and I suggest you always err on the lighter side of what you require. If the filler is not dark enough it can be darkened using a little stain after it has dried (see Chapter 12).

Once you have chosen your colour, simply smear the filler into the scratch or blemish using your fingers, a knife or other suitable

Fig 11.11 A can of stopping.

instrument. It is always best to overfill; excess can be sanded down after it is dry using fine wet-and-dry.

The drawback with this type of filler is that it has no strength and is consequently useless for filling corners, edges and large areas of damage. Such repairs should be carried out using . . .

CAR BODY FILLER

This filler is available from any car accessory shop, and can be used to fill, mould and re-create whole sections of carving. Once mixed with its hardener, it will harden in between 5 and 30 minutes depending on the amount of hardener used. While the filler is still 'curing' you can carve it with a sharp knife. It will stick to wood like a shipwrecked sailor, and is therefore perfect for restoring damaged corners and chipped edges. When it has gone very hard, you can use wet-and-dry paper to make it as smooth as marble.

A further bonus with this material is that it hardens enough for you to copy the texture of the surrounding wood grain into it using a knife or needle.

For complicated jobs, this filler can be progressively built up and carved back, and, as you now know, can also be used to cast replacement finials (see page 63).

One drawback is that car body filler is only available in one colour – light grey – so it is essential that once it is dried it is stained (see page 90 for information on how to do this). Fig 11.12 shows the process of making a repair using car body filler.

The other drawback is the smell. This filler has a pungent chemical odour which can make some people feel nauseous and cause eyes to smart. Always ensure good ventilation during use, and wear a mask to protect against the dust generated when rubbing the material down.

PLASTIC WOOD

This material is designed for use by carpenters and decorators who will subsequently paint over it. It is too coarse in texture to be of any use to the restorer.

SAWDUST AND GLUE

Sawdust and glue is widely rumoured to be the best wood filler available this side of Pluto, the idea being that you make your own filler by mixing wood dust with glue. This is an old French-polisher's trick that relies on using animal glue (see Chapter 2) and very fine wood dust. If you do not use animal glue on a regular basis, it is best avoided.

REPAIRING THE FOOT OF A TABLE

Fig 11.12(a) The foot of the table has been gnawed mercilessly by a teething puppy. Because of the amount of filler needed and the likelihood of the foot being knocked in its future life, car body filler is a very good choice for the repair. To give the filler extra grip, you can see that I inserted two 1in (25mm) nails into the wood.

Fig 11.12(b) First, the filler is roughly moulded to shape.

Fig 11.12(c) A second application of filler then fills in the finer details.

Fig 11.12(d) Finally, the filler is sanded using fine-grade abrasive paper (wear a mask) until it is as smooth as marble and ready for staining.

12
STAINS

One of the easiest and quickest ways to change the appearance of a piece of furniture is to use a stain.

There are four main groups of stains traditionally used for colouring wood:

- Water stains.
- Chemical stains.
- Oil stains.
- Spirit stains (also known as aniline dyes).

If you are a beginner, start by becoming conversant with oil and spirit stains. Water stains are similar in application to spirit stains, but because the solvent for them is water they can cause adverse reactions in some woods as well as raising the grain as a matter of course. Chemical stains are frequently highly toxic, and are not recommended. Consequently I have concentrated on oil and spirit stains here.

OIL STAINS

A wide range of oil stains is available from DIY stores, and have been specifically mixed by their manufacturers with the amateur DIY user in mind. They usually come in rectangular tins, and most shops usually display about 12 different colours.

These colours often have fancy names; do try to think of them in terms of their actual colour and not be swayed by the names. Equally, the ticket attached to the tin should only be regarded as a rough colour guide. The best way to find the colour you want is to take the stain from the shelf, give it a thorough shaking, unscrew the top and look at its underside (see Fig 12.1). The clear plastic insert normally present there will be coated with a thin layer of the stain, and this represents its true colour. This, in combination with the colour of your wood, will produce the final result. The best way to gain an 'eye' for the right colour stain is by experimenting on spare pieces of wood.

You may also encounter a colour chart showing the effects of stains on pieces of wood. The woods used for such charts tend to be light-coloured, such as pine or birch; bear this in mind if you are about to buy a stain with which to colour a dark wood – the result will be very different.

*Fig 12.1 To judge the true colour of a stain, look at the colour on
the inside of the tin's cap.*

The range of colours sold in this type of stain is quite limited; there are no bright yellows, greens or blues. However, such stains are usually light fast, meaning they will not fade in strong sunlight, which is a very important attribute for a stain.

Oil stains are intermixable, but if you decide to mix a particular colour for your project, make sure you mix more than enough; if you run out before the job is over you will find it very difficult to achieve a perfect colour match.

Staining is one of the few processes in woodfinishing that is almost irreversible. It is possible to remove some of the stain if you have made a mistake, but removing it all will mean sanding away the top 0.5mm of wood.

ACHIEVING THE RIGHT COLOUR MATCH

It is far better to get the right colour first time. There is a method for this, and here it is.

1 Experiment on a piece of scrap wood similar in colour to your project. Make the scrap as large as possible and stand it next to the project.
2 Make a number of colour tests if you need to, and whatever you do, do not proceed until you have the right colour.
3 If you intend your project to live in a particular colour environment, take your test-wood there and give further consideration to the best and most harmonious colour choice.

Remember that the 'colour when wet is the colour you get'. When you first apply the stain it will be wet and much darker than when it dries out, but this is the colour you will see once a finish has been applied. Give your tester pieces a coat or two of varnish so that they permanently represent the finished colour.

It is also worth remembering that unstained wood will also turn a few shades darker when a finish is applied; before you decide to stain, wet the wood with some white spirit or meths to see what colour the natural wood would go were it given a clear finish (see Fig 12.2).

THE DISADVANTAGE OF OIL STAINS

The best way to demonstrate this is for you to carry out a little experiment. Take a piece of scrap wood, scratch it across the grain and then hit it a couple of times with a hammer to bruise the wood (see Fig 12.3). Now apply some dark stains to the surface with a cloth or brush and wipe off the excess.

The problem then becomes obvious; any scratch, bruise, dent, area of rough surface or chip will become aggressively highlighted by the stain 'gathering' at the point of injury (see Fig 12.4). Such injuries

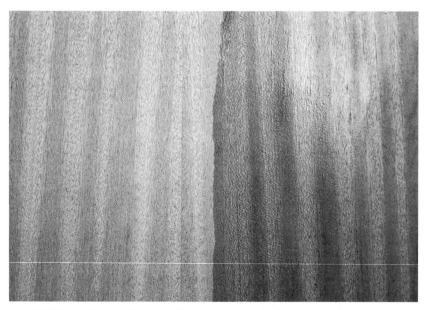

Fig 12.2 The results of opting for a clear finish rather than a stain can be viewed 'in advance' by wiping over the surface with white spirit.

Fig 12.3 Damaged wood before the application of an oil stain . . .

Fig 12.4 . . . and afterwards. You can see how the blemishes have been highlighted by the stain.

can be numerous on old or neglected furniture, and become eyesores with the injudicious application of a stain.

APPLYING OIL STAINS

PREPARATION
Before applying an oil stain, check over your project for defects and try to get rid of as many as possible. Areas of roughness can be scraped or sanded down, as can places where old glue still adheres. Look very carefully for these, as dried glue can be almost invisible. Repair and fill dents and deep scratches, and look closely for any of the old finish which still remains and must be removed.

Fig 12.5 An even application of stain shows clearly how end grain stains much darker than the rest of the wood.

As an insurance you may choose to apply what I call a 'discloser stain'. To do this, rub a thin coat of stain over the wood in a superficial manner to disclose any surface injuries, which can then be repaired.

Remember that end grain is much more absorbent than the rest of the timber, and as a result absorbs more of the pigments contained in the stain, making it much darker (see Fig 12.5). All pieces of furniture contain end grain, and the successful application of an oil stain depends on identifying these areas and making sure you do not saturate them with stain (see Fig 12.6).

APPLICATION

You do not have to stain and finish areas such as the insides of drawers or the undersides, but if you choose to do so remember these areas will also need a couple of coats of finish over the stain to prevent it leaching and staining the eventual contents.

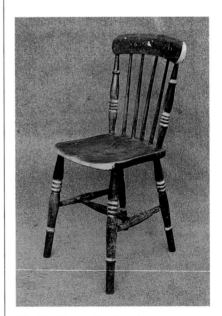

Fig 12.6 Areas of end grain are highlighted in yellow on this chair.

1 Remember to wear old clothes to protect against splashes.

2 Shake the can vigorously for two or three minutes, as much of the pigment in the oil stain will have settled to the bottom of the can.

3 Take a cotton cloth, cover the opening of the can with cloth and forefinger, and spill a small and controlled amount of stain on to the cloth.

4 Rub the stain into the wood, working methodically around the piece, staining one section (such as a leg or side) before moving on to the next, until the whole project is covered.

5 Treat the end grain last, and when your cloth is almost dry, rub it into the end grain. This makes it impossible to overdo the amount of stain you apply to these areas.

If you darken the end grain too much, you can improve things by rubbing the affected area with a cloth soaked in white spirit. This also works if you find a 'gathering' around an area that is damaged or contains some wayward grain. White spirit, as you have probably guessed, is the thinner for oil stains, and therefore dilutes their colour, making them weaker.

It follows from this that any product that can be thinned with white spirit can be tinted and coloured with oil stains – for example, polyurethane varnishes, waxes and oil based finishes can all be coloured in this way. This mixing facility is extremely useful, as you will see in the chapters that follow.

SPIRIT STAINS

These are less readily available than oil stains, but can be obtained from specialist suppliers of woodfinishing products. They are also known as aniline dyes, and come in either powder form or ready-mixed. Powders simply require the addition of meths to make them soluble. I prefer to buy them in powder form, as this allows you to mix dozens of colour strengths and makes the stains much more versatile (see Fig 12.7).

There is a far greater range of spirit stains than oil stains; they are made in all colours of the spectrum, also allowing much greater flexibility.

Fig 12.7 From tea wash to dark coffee – some of the tones that can be mixed from one spirit stain powder. The colour you get depends on how much meths you use when mixing.

APPLICATION

Spirit stains are best brushed on. Be careful not to flick the brush or the stain will travel undesirably great distances. By the same token remember to cover any vulnerable items around you and to wear old clothes for the job.

Because spirit stains have a meths base they dry very quickly. This can be a drawback because if the stain dries too quickly during application, the first coat will be inadvertently overlapped by a second coat. Some areas will end up with two coats, resulting in unsightly dark marks.

To avoid this, do not apply spirit stains in hot and dry surroundings and always try to keep a 'wet edge' to the stain when it is being applied. This is fairly easy when staining small items, but larger pieces need to be stained in small sections at a time, each section being completely finished before moving on to the next.

Table tops and cupboards are best tackled by first brushing on a coat of meths which will wet the wood and keep it from drying out too quickly. However, bear in mind that meths contains water, and there is therefore a danger of grain raising. Sometimes it helps to enlist another pair of hands for staining very large areas; one of you brushes on the thin coats of meths while the other follows behind applying the stain.

Because spirit stains are meths based, they can be mixed with French polishes. This leads to many useful applications, particularly the staining and texturing of filled areas.

STAINING AND TEXTURING FILLED AREAS

Spirit stains can also be used to colour areas that have been filled (see pages 80–3). If you used a filler that matches the colour of the wood to repair a blemish, this will usually be enough to deceive the eye, but larger repairs need to be colour-enhanced to mimic the surrounding wood and look effective.

Try the following method:

1   Before applying the first base coat of spirit stain, seal the filler with two thin coats of French polish to stop the spirit stain soaking into the filler, so making the brushing of fine lines much more precise (see Fig 12.8). French polish also acts as a barrier between stain and filler, allowing for errors should they occur. So, if you make a mistake you can easily clean it off with meths and wire wool without causing any discoloration to the surrounding wood. At the same

Fig 12.8 Using spirit stain to camouflage a repair: the first coat of
spirit stain has been applied over a sealing coat of French polish.

time, if you do a perfect job, you
can then seal your work with
French polish, giving a lasting
finish.

2 Copy the texture of the
surrounding wood using a
needle, pin or craft knife to
scratch into the filler (see Fig
12.9).

3 Apply another coat of French
polish.

4 Mix a base colour spirit stain,
making it the same colour and
tone as the lightest colour in the
surrounding wood.

5 Brush this on to the surface and
evaluate its effects on the wood.
Should it be darker? redder?
browner? lighter?

6 Depending on what you decide,
either add some colour or
remove some using wire wool.
For pinpoint accuracy, wrap the
wire wool around a cotton bud
or a matchstick.

7 Now examine the surrounding
colours and try to mix the next
darkest colour. This next colour
is often made up by simply
adding more of the same
powdered stain to your existing
colour. Apply this over the top of
the base colour with an artist's
brush in grain-shaped strokes,
which will help enhance the
texture.

8 Soften any brush strokes and
mistakes with wire wool.

Fig 12.9 Applying some texture and grain effect by scratching the filler with a pin or knife.

9   Now mix the darkest colours and paint these flecks in with deft strokes of the brush. If you make a mistake or want to rub anything out, use the wire wool as an eraser.

10 Once finished, give the whole lot a couple of coats of French polish to seal it all in (see Fig 12.10).

This method of building up and cutting back until the right effect is achieved requires much patience but is well worth all the effort. It can be used on all French-polished work, on bare wood before polishing, or when disguising filler that has been used to repair scratches in French polish. The most effective method is to apply the stains in between each layer of French polish, sandwiching the colour between successive layers of polish.

You can use this technique for small areas of wood that are due to have other finishes (besides French polish) applied over the top, but it is always preferable for larger filled sections to use colours and finishes that are compatible with the final finish.

For polyurethane varnish finishes, you can use artists' oil paints on filler to camouflage defects and then seal your handiwork in with a couple of coats of polyurethane varnish. Alternatively, if the grain of the surrounding wood is not too complicated and you do not need to use much artistry, you can use oil stains mixed with a little varnish.

Spirit stains can be mixed with cellulose finishes in the same way as they are used with French polish, but experiment for compatibility before you spend too much time 'creating'.

COLOUR AND HOW TO MIX IT

There are three primary colours: yellow, red, and blue. These are pure colours and cannot be created by mixing other colours together.

There are three secondary colours: orange, purple and green. These are obtained by mixing the primary colours.

To make orange, mix yellow and red.

To make purple, mix red and blue.

To make green, mix yellow and blue.

Brown is a notable omission here, and is of course an important colour to the furniture restorer. Browns are achieved by mixing a primary colour with the opposite secondary colour on the 'colour wheel' (see Fig 12.11). Therefore, mixing red and green, yellow and purple, or orange and blue will all produce a brown.

Knowledge of the colour wheel is indispensable to furniture restorers. It tells them, for example, that a red-colour mahogany wood can be turned browner by adding a little green to a French-polish finish.

Fig 12.10 The finished result.

Fig 12.11 The colour wheel.

Here are some old-time French-polishers' recipes for colours mixed with spirit stain, using black, yellow and red.

Dark oak 6 parts black, 1½ parts yellow, 1 part red

Middle oak 4 parts black, 3 parts yellow, 2 parts red

Brown walnut 3 parts black, 2 parts yellow, 2 parts red

Grey walnut 10 parts black, 1 part yellow, thin down

Green walnut 4 parts black, 1 part yellow

Mahogany 14 parts red, 3 parts black, 2 parts yellow

Rosewood 2 parts red, 1 part black

All these can be thinned down with meths to the required tone. If you want to mix colours for use with white-spirit-soluble finishes, you can use artists' oil paints.

13
WAXES

Waxing is one of the oldest and simplest processes for finishing woodwork, and as such is always a good 'starter finish' if you are new to restoration.

Wax finishes need to be maintained by a periodic 'topping up' of wax as the finish is removed by wear and tear, or is absorbed gradually into the timber, or is decayed by heat and water. How frequently a wax finish needs repolishing depends on the amount of use it gets. As a piece ages and the number of wax applications increases, so does the depth and colour of the finish.

The full character of a wax finish is best illustrated by looking at old waxed chairs (see Fig 13.1). Those

Fig 13.1 Two examples of the character of a wax finish. The patina due to age can clearly be seen on the seat of the top chair, and around the base of the slats of the bottom chair.

areas constantly polished by use (backs and seats) achieve a very high shine, while the stretchers and the legs become dull and dark as dirt becomes embedded in the wax. This is an unmistakable feature of antique furniture, and highly prized by collectors as an indication of age.

A drawback of wax finishes is that they are slightly sticky and do attract dirt. Classic historical examples of this are Tudor furniture, some of which is almost black due to soot from chimneys then positioned in the middle of the room. By Jacobean times the chimney had been moved to the side of the room, and much furniture from the late sixteenth century has a dark brown patina, rather than a black patina, as a result. Because of its need for frequent topping up, and its inherent sticky qualities, wax polish is not recommended for use in food cupboards or on beds. Wax polish can be damaged by heat, water and prolonged exposure to direct sunlight, so avoid using it in kitchens, bathrooms or outside.

Wax polish is nonetheless a very beautiful finish and very easy to apply, requiring little skill, and its ability to be rejuvenated rather than stripped and refinished is a major advantage.

OBTAINING WAX

You can make your own. Beeswax is easily dissolved by turpentine and the judicious application of heat. Should you decide to try this,

Fig 13.2 Polishing up a surface with wax polish. Photograph courtesy of Liberon Waxes Ltd.

beware – turpentine is highly flammable and heat is hot! A recipe for making your own wax polish appears on page 98.

You can buy wax ready-made from your DIY store, and you will find it comes in two main types: aerosol spray and non-aerosol spray. The spray version contains a cleaning agent designed to clean a range of surfaces from formica to the television. It is not suitable as a method of applying a wax finish to bare wood, nor for cleaning and polishing furniture with a long-established wax finish, because some of the chemicals in the spray can dissolve the old wax, thereby removing it.

Non-aerosol waxes come in tins or glass pots and have a butter-like consistency. They are basic preparations containing in the simplest of cases just beeswax and turpentine (see Fig 13.2).

There is often a choice of coloured waxes, and those produced in darker colours have come to be known as 'antique' waxes. These are not usually needed, especially if you are a beginner. It is much better to colour the wood using a stain and then wax it.

Antique or coloured wax can be useful if you are patching a damaged area (see Chapter 11) but I still feel it is better to buy a clear wax, from which you can mix all the other types of wax preparation (see page 99).

APPLICATION

METHOD 1

You will require some clear, uncoloured wax and half a dozen soft, clean, cotton cloths free of buttons, threads or zips. If you have sensitive skin, always wear protective gloves. Remember that turpentine is flammable and gives off strong fumes. Keep a window or door open and keep the work away from naked flames or cigarettes.

1   Dip a cloth into the wax mixture and apply a generous coating of wax to the piece, rubbing it firmly into the wood.
2   Do not remove the surplus wax, but keep rubbing it around and around, pushing it into the grain of the wood.
3   Leave the piece for two hours with the build-up of wax on the surface, to allow it to be absorbed into the fibres, and the turpentine to evaporate, leaving the solid part of the mix – the beeswax – behind.
4   After the two hours, take the same cloth and start all over again, rubbing in the hardened wax with fresh wax.
5   Now take a fresh cloth and rub

the excess wax off the furniture. You will probably find you will need at least two if not three fresh cloths by the end. Polish the wood as hard as you can to remove all traces of loose wax. To check, pull your clean (unwaxed) index finger over the surface of the wood as if you were drawing a figure one. If this leaves a noticeable smear, then there is still some loose polish to be removed.

You may have to repeat the above process several times before a satisfactory finish begins to appear – this very much depends on the type of wood being waxed.

If the piece you are working on has some intricate mouldings, use thinned down 'liquid wax'(see page 99 for a recipe), which can be brushed into complicated areas with a 3in (76mm) decorator's paint brush and then polished using a shoe-cleaning brush. If a lot of thick wax accumulates in awkward areas, wrap cloth around the tip of a lollipop stick, and cut the stick to the required shape using a sharp knife.

Method 2

This method is a little easier because it builds up the shine quicker. In addition, once applied it does not need as much maintenance, and is more resistant to grime. Some craftspeople prefer Method 1 however, as they feel it results in a deeper and better finish.

1 Thin some French polish (colour of your choosing) with methylated spirit to a ratio of 1:1. Use this to seal the wood, applying it evenly and thinly using a brush, and allowing half an hour's drying time before adding a second coat. You can also buy proprietary sealers, or use thinned-down polyurethane varnish, Danish oil or teak oil as a sealer.

2 Leave for two hours before rubbing down with a medium-to-fine grade of wire wool. Dust off loose fibres left behind by the wool, and the piece will be ready for waxing.

3 Now follow the instructions for Method 1, and you will find the shine will build up much quicker and easier.

HOW TO MIX YOUR OWN WAX POLISH

Always remember to allow sufficient ventilation and guard against fire.

1 Melt some pure beeswax into a double boiler (one saucepan inside another is adequate; see Fig 13.3).

Fig 13.3 The double boiler method for mixing your own wax polish.

2 Remove from the heat.
3 Add an equal quantity of pure turpentine.
4 Return to the heat, stirring constantly, and then pour into a suitable receptacle to set.

THINNING DOWN WAX

Thinned wax (sometimes called liquid wax) can be bought ready-made but it is cheaper and more convenient to make it yourself from ordinary wax by adding turpentine or white spirit.

Simply spoon a little wax into a lidded jar, add a small quantity of white spirit and shake vigorously. To transform this into a cream wax, add a little warm water to the thinned wax, and a couple of drops of washing up liquid, and then shake once again.

Your personalized range of wax finishes can be further customized by adding colour as you require it using oil stains or artist's oils (see Chapter 12).

REMOVING WAX FINISHES

Wax finishes can be removed sympathetically, preserving the patina in much the same way as the antiquikstrip method described in Chapter 8, by cleaning it off with wire wool soaked in turps or white spirit.

CLEANING WAX FINISHES

Wipe them with a cloth slightly dampened with white spirit. This will soften the wax and allow the cloth to polish it and lift off the surface dirt. You can also use a cream wax which you can make yourself, as described on this page.

14
OIL FINISHES

There are several types of oil finish used in furniture restoration:

▌ Danish oil.
▌ Raw linseed oil.
▌ Boiled linseed oil.
▌ Tung oil.
▌ Teak oil.
▌ Edible oils.

They all have the following in common:

▌ The same oily constitution.
▌ The same method of application.
▌ The same common thinners – white spirit.

The difference between them lies in the number of applications required to constitute a finish, their respective drying times, and their resilience to wear and tear.

SAFETY

Always treat the rags used for the application of oil finishes with great care; they have the potential to spontaneously combust. Dispose of such rags safely, or, if you want to use them again, drape them over a bench or better still, hang them up outside on a washing line. Once they are dry they will be perfectly safe.

APPLICATION

The method of application for oil finishes is the same whichever finish you have decided to use.

1 Rub the oil into the wood.
2 Once dry, apply another coat.
3 When the wood will not accept any more oil, the finish is complete.

Different oils will require different numbers of coats before saturation is complete. Traditional linseed oil finishes can take up to 30 applications, with weeks between while they dry, whereas with Danish oil, two coats may be enough, with only around four hours between each coat.

THE TYPES OF OIL

DANISH OIL

A very good finish for the beginner, this is the quickest and easiest of all the oil finishes, while at the same time giving you a taste of the basic methods involved in the application of them all.

Danish oil is brushed on to the wood and allowed to soak in for two or three minutes, before being rubbed with a clean lint-free cotton cloth to absorb the excess. If the oil becomes too sticky, dampen the cloth with a little white spirit. Typically, end grain will need three coats to every one coat on the ordinary grain.

If you have stained the wood, thin the first coat of oil with white spirit, apply this with a decorator's paint brush, and wipe off any excess or drips with a cloth. Do not rub this coat as this will remove the stain from the surface and create lighter patches.

Leave this coat to dry hard (this takes about four hours), and then rub the surface with wet-and-dry paper to remove any dust particles or rough patches. Then apply a second coat in exactly the same way. You can repeat this process many times but you should find that two or three coats will be sufficient. More than this causes a build-up of oil on the surface which will give the wood a glossy finish. This gloss can be removed by rubbing the affected area with wire wool soaked in white spirit and finishing off with a soft cloth.

Danish oil is ideal for outdoor use, and on furniture needing protection from damp, heat and weather, such as kitchen, bathroom, conservatory and garden furniture. I also recommend it for external-facing doors and garden gates. Apply a 'top-up' coat to external wood every 18 to 36 months, depending on the weather and whether movable items are brought inside during the winter. Simply rub down the wood with fine sandpaper and wipe or brush another coat on.

This oil is also excellent for providing a seal prior to the application of a high-gloss wax finish (see Chapter 13).

OIL FROM ANOTHER COUNTRY

You can make a similar concoction to Danish oil yourself. I call it 'oil from another country'. This is applied in the same way as Danish oil and to similar effect, and is also a useful way of using up leftover polyurethane varnish.

Make it from one part linseed oil, one part polyurethane varnish (outdoor varnish if intended for use out of doors) and one part white spirit. Pour the ingredients into a pot and stir.

LINSEED OIL FINISHES

Some craftspeople swear by it, while others swear at it. Suffice it to say that the full traditional linseed oil finish is a contentious subject.

Linseed oil and similar vegetable oils have been used consistently throughout man's involvement with wood, because, until recently, it was the only finish that was capable of protecting wooden items used outside, or protecting items which are subject to much abuse. It remains a common finish for garden furniture and dining tables.

When applied to interior furniture, linseed oil has the advantages of being heat-, scratch-, water- and alcohol-resistant, and is easily and quickly repaired in cases of hard wear or neglect. These must be tempered with the fact that this finish is not very durable, and hence needs regular maintenance.

Fig 14.1 The tissue test. When there is little or no oil left on the tissue after wiping, you are ready for the next coat.

It is however very easy to apply, and once it has soaked into the wood it will typically take on a soft-lustre finish.

APPLICATION

This is the same as for any oil. Each coat requires thorough rubbing to push the oil into the fibres of the wood.

You need to apply many coats of this oil, and each coat will take much longer to dry than other oil preparations. To test to see if it is dry enough to apply the next coat, wipe a paper tissue over the surface to see if any of the oil is still wet (see Fig 14.1).

An old-time guide to linseed oil application may make the problem clearer:

- Apply one coat every hour for a day.
- Then once a day for a week.
- Then once a week for a month.
- Then once a month for a year.
- Then once every six months for the rest of the piece's life.

During application and drying this oil will emit an all-pervading smell, which, over time, can become obnoxious. As you can imagine, over the centuries, many methods have been devised to try and speed up this process of linseed oil application, or at least make it more user-friendly. For example, you can warm the oil, or thin it with turpentine, so that it penetrates the fibres of the wood more easily, or you can use boiled linseed oil bought from the DIY store. This has been boiled and 'doctored' to produce a quicker drying but thicker oil.

Approach linseed oil finishing with caution, but if you have the time and patience to try it out, do give it a go, as a properly applied linseed oil finish can look extremely beautiful.

CHINESE TUNG OIL

Pure Chinese tung oil can be expensive and is hard to come by in the UK, but I have heard very good

Fig 14.2 A tin of 'finishing' oil. This is a common proprietary brand, similar to Danish oil. Photograph courtesy of Liberon Waxes Ltd.

reports about it from the USA. In the UK it is relatively unknown. Many of the other proprietary oil mixes include a measure of tung oil in their constitutions.

TEAK OIL

This substance is a proprietary mix designed to apply a finish to teak wood. Teak is a very hard and durable wood, much used in marine environments because it contains its own naturally occurring oils. Because of these oils, teak can cause difficulties when applying other types of finish. Therefore, the traditional finish for teak is teak oil.

However, it is not commonly known that teak oil works very well on other timbers. It is relatively quick-drying and will leave a slightly shinier finish than Danish oil.

SUNFLOWER AND OTHER EDIBLE OILS

A number of edible oils, such as sunflower, olive and corn oil, are used for cooking, and are most commonly found on woodwork found in the kitchen, such as salad bowls and chopping boards. They are not intended to be very durable, and are often rubbed in after washing up to maintain a piece's look and a level of protection.

15
FRENCH POLISHING

The idea that French polishing is an impossibly skilled craft has been fostered and encouraged for years by craftspeople and furniture restorers who earn their living from this particular skill.

The truth is, with careful instruction and a little practice, there is no reason why even an absolute beginner should not get very good results, first time.

WHAT IS IT?

French polish is based on a naturally occurring substance, which is produced in Asia where it is harvested from a particular type of aphid-like insect, *Laccifer lacca*. Part of this creature's lifecycle involves exuding and eventually entombing itself in a thick, toffee-like substance, also known as shellac, and this is the raw material from which French polishes are made.

Shellac has the very useful property of becoming liquid when mixed with methylated spirit, and hardening again after the meths has evaporated.

PROS AND CONS

PROS

- One bottle of French polish can produce a wide range of finishes, from a dull matt sealer to a glass-like high gloss.
- It is the *authentic* finish for many antiques.
- Many craftspeople consider it the most beautiful finish available.
- The final finish can be as good as expensive modern spray finishes, and yet the equipment required for French polishing costs very little.

CONS

- Easily damaged by scratching.
- Decomposes and is marked by heat.
- Dissolved by alcohol.
- Application is time-consuming.

FRENCH POLISHING WITH A RUBBER

There are several methods of applying French polish, and I refer to these as recipes. This one is not the quickest way to apply French polish, nor the simplest, but it does teach you the basic principles of French polishing, and produces a classic high-gloss finish, also known as a 'mirror finish' or 'piano finish'.

This is the most difficult form of French polishing and many other French polish recipes are derived from it. If you master this recipe, the others will be easy.

PREPARATION

THE TESTER

First, practise on a suitable piece of wood, such as an offcut of veneered chipboard or plywood, about 12–18in square (305–457mm). This tester piece is important and should be kept for future experiments with other French polishing techniques.

OBTAINING THE MATERIALS

You will need:

- Suitably coloured French polish.
- Four pieces of 100% cotton cloth between 9 and 12in (229 and 305mm) square. I prefer curtain lining, but old handkerchiefs, bedsheets and shirts are all possible sources.
- A quantity of cotton wool.
- An eggcupful of raw linseed oil.
- A wide-brimmed container with a screw top to store rubbers between sessions.

- Meths.
- 600 grit wet-and-dry paper.
- A clean piece of thick paper.

You are likely to find three types of French polish at your DIY shop: button polish, white polish and French polish (see Fig 15.1). From the point of view of the novice restorer, the only difference between these is their colour.

White polish is a light creamy colour intended for use on light-coloured woods. Button polish is orangey-brown for use on light brown or orange-toned woods, and French polish is a dark brown colour for use on dark woods. Always avoid using old polish, because it can take a long time to dry.

Fig 15.1 White polish, home-made button polish, and French polish.

MAKING A RUBBER

This is a traditional French-polisher's tool made from cotton material and cotton wool. It is used to apply the French polish in thin, even coats.

First, organize your workspace and cover your bench with the thick, clean paper, giving you somewhere clinically clean to make and fill the rubber, as follows. You will find the whole process easier if the cotton wool and material are wet with methylated spirits, as this will stop the rubber springing open all the time.

1   Take a piece of cotton material and fold it into a pad about 5in

Fig 15.2 Fold a piece of cotton material into a pad about 5in (127mm) square.

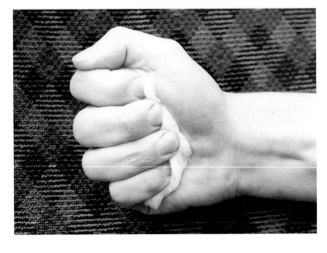

Fig 15.3 Squeeze a large enough ball of cotton wool in your hand so that your fingertips just touch your palm.

(127mm) square (see Fig 15.2).

2 Take enough cotton wool in your hand so that when you squeeze the ball in your fist, your fingertips just touch the palm of your hand (see Fig 15.3).

3 Place this wad of cotton wool in the middle of the square of cotton material, and mould it roughly into an egg shape (see Fig 15.4).

4 Wrap this egg shape tightly in the pad of cotton material by drawing in the pad's four corners, and hold the corners tightly in the middle with one finger. This is known as a fad, and should be the shape of a diamond (see Fig 15.5).

Fig 15.4 Place the cotton wool in the middle of the cotton square and mould it into an egg shape.

Fig 15.5 The fad.

5 Adjust the size of the fad or the size of the egg as required to make a tight package.

6 Take another piece of cotton material and lay it flat on the clean scrap of wood or paper.

Place the fad in the centre of the material with the top of the diamond pointing into one corner. Then move it 1in (25mm) closer towards that corner (see Fig 15.6).

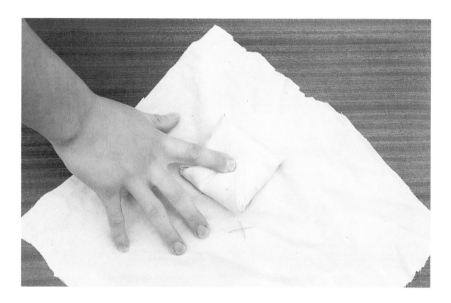

Fig 15.6 Place the fad in the centre of the material, and then move it 1in (25mm) closer to a corner, as shown.

Fig 15.7 Pull up the sides of the outer material around the fad.

7 Gather any loose material above the fad and twist the loose material a number of times to hold everything in place (see Figs 15.7 and 15.8).

8 Your rubber should now look something like that shown in Fig 15.9, and feel very firm to the touch.

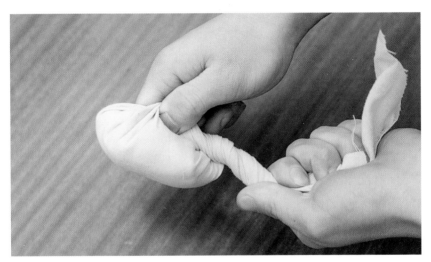

Fig 15.8 Twist the loose material above the fad.

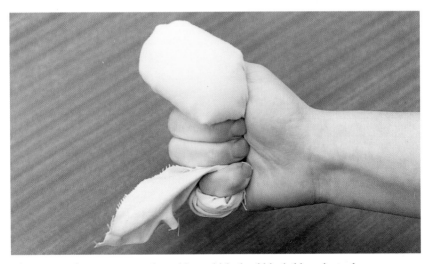

Fig 15.9 You have now created a rubber, which should be held as shown here.

Fig 15.10 Your rubber will at some point wear out. Inspect the sole regularly, and move the outer cloth as soon as a hole is found.

The complete rubber is commonly referred to as a 'shoe' because of its shape, and this term is useful for referring to various parts of the rubber.

It is from the sole of the rubber that the French polish is delivered, so it is important that there are no creases or bits of dirt attaching themselves to that area. Check the rubber after each pass, as the presence of any foreign body could damage the finish. In the first stages of French polishing, the rubber may wear out quickly due to the roughness of the bare wood. If this happens, reposition the fad to another corner of the outer material (see Fig 15.10).

Rubbers can be made as large or small as you require; as small as your fingertip to get into awkward nooks and crannies, or as large as your hand to polish a boardroom table.

The rubber performs a variety of essential functions. It filters the French polish so that no foreign bodies find their way to the sole and scratch the surface or become embedded in the finish; it applies a very thin coat of polish to the wood; and the abrasive quality of the cotton cloth burnishes every coat of polish as it is applied, not just the final coat, as we do with rubbing compounds on other coating finishes.

HOLDING THE RUBBER

Hold the rubber firmly in your hand so that it cannot 'rock and roll' on the surface of the wood. Grip it tightly at the base of the twisted gathered material (refer to Fig 15.9).

CHARGING THE RUBBER

1 Mix some polish and methylated spirit in equal quantities in a container, giving a 50/50 mix of thin French polish.

2 Open the rubber and pour a liberal quantity of polish into the cotton wool. Don't overdo it, but be sure to use enough so that the polish soaks into the cotton wool and into the outer cloth (see Fig 15.11).

3 Wrap up the rubber and squeeze it so that the French polish oozes through the cotton covering.

4 Rub this around on your clean scrap wood to distribute the polish around the sole. Ideally you need an even distribution of polish oozing from the sole, with no dry spots and no areas that are too wet. If the rubber is too wet, rub it around on your thick paper or scrap wood to dry it out a bit (see Fig 15.12).

Experience will teach you that a wet rubber needs only slight downward pressure to release a thin coating of polish. As the rubber dries, more pressure is required until a lot of pressure is needed to release an almost non-existent film of polish.

Ideally you are aiming to begin with a wet rubber which applies the polish but does not need much pressure, and, as the rubber dries and you apply more pressure, you will also be burnishing the polish that has already been applied. This interplay between the application of very thin films of French polish and

*Fig 15.11
Charging the
rubber.*

Fig 15.12 The ideal distribution of polish on the rubber.

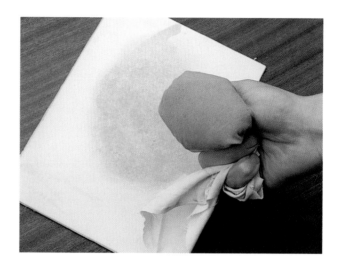

the burnishing of previously deposited polish is the essence of French polishing.

BEFORE YOU BEGIN

Before you begin polishing, it is important that the temperature and moisture of the air are right. French polish in a damp environment and you run the risk of the polish absorbing some of the moisture from the air, which will result in a cloudy-white discoloration of the polish. If the atmosphere is too cold, the polish will take too long to dry and be difficult to work. Ideally, the conditions should be warm and dry.

The wood you are working on should also be warm and dry. Do not bring your project in from a cold, damp garage or outhouse and work on it straight away. Give it time to 'acclimatize'. If you French polish cold wood in warm surroundings, the minute quantities of air contained in the wood will eventually expand underneath the finish and cause tiny unwanted bubbles in the surface of the wood.

THE FIRST PASS

Starting in a top corner, polish the rubber over the wood in small circular motions, moving it along in the same direction as the grain. When you reach the other end, move the rubber down a couple of inches and, still with small circular motions and without stopping, move back in the other direction (see Fig 15.13(a)).

Try not to touch the area of polish that you have just deposited on the wood, as it will be starting to dry and getting tacky. Continue on

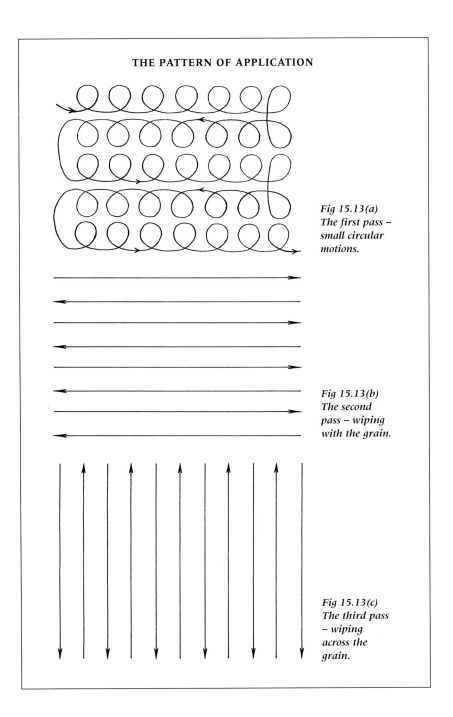

THE PATTERN OF APPLICATION

Fig 15.13(a)
The first pass –
small circular
motions.

Fig 15.13(b)
The second
pass – wiping
with the grain.

Fig 15.13(c)
The third pass
– wiping
across the
grain.

in the same pattern as a farmer would plough a field, moving up and down until the whole piece of wood has received an even coat of polish. The first pass is now complete. It may not be perfect, but you will have plenty of opportunities to improve it. Your goal is always to apply a very thin coat of polish to the wood as evenly as possible.

When making a pass do not under any circumstances stop the rubber on the surface. When you lift the rubber off the surface it must be moving, and the same applies to when it is returned to the surface. Get into the habit of making a swiping action when you start and when you finish a pass. If you stop on the surface, the rubber will redissolve the finish and you will blemish the polish.

THE SECOND PASS

Wait for the first pass to dry (about 30 seconds) and then begin the second. This is made in a wiping action moving with the grain, starting at the top corner. Wipe the rubber over the surface. Start your wiping action a few inches beyond the wood and then lower it down to land on the edge of the tester, just like a child pretending to land a toy aeroplane. This will ensure that the rubber is never stationary on the surface. When you reach the other end of the tester you can 'lift off'.

Now repeat the same action, and this time try to get the wipe as close as possible to the previous one without touching it. Keep repeating this all the way down the wood until the whole surface is covered (see Fig 15.13(b)). If you miss a bit don't go back and re-do it – the rubber will stick to the polish and the pass will be ruined. Just make a mental note to cover the missed stop on the next pass. A common tendency with beginners is to 'take off' and 'land' too late, leaving dry patches near the edges. If this becomes a problem, sneak in some 'rogue' passes when the previous pass has dried, that just cover the patches you have missed.

THE THIRD PASS

Wait for the second pass to dry before proceeding to the next. This pass is made in exactly the same way as the second pass except that it goes across the grain instead of with the grain (see Fig 15.13(c)). The reason for this is to ensure a smooth and even surface which is not streaky or stripey, as it would be if you only made passes in one direction. If you make a bad pass in one direction and leave a noticeable pattern in the finish, miss out that particular pass for the next couple of goes.

THE FOURTH PASS

This is made in the same way as the first pass, and so the cycle continues. After about six passes you will begin to see a shine developing. The degree of shine will depend on the type of wood and the thickness of the polish used. After about 12 to 24 passes you should have built up enough polish on the surface to create a shine. The surface will also start to become sticky, making it harder for the rubber to glide over the surface. At this point you should stop. The first session is complete.

SUMMARY

1 Always work in a warm, dry environment, on warm, dry projects.
2 Remember; the principle of French polishing is to deposit many very thin coats of polish evenly on the surface.
3 Never stop the rubber on the surface.
4 Look after the edges, and the middle will look after itself.
5 If you make a mistake, wait until it has dried overnight, and then rub back the offending area with wet-and-dry.

6 Always ensure the rubber is moving when it makes contact with and breaks contact with the wood.
7 Check the face of the rubber frequently for dirt, tears or creases.
8 Alternate between the three passes. When you become more confident, make up your own passes in response to the way the finish is evolving and the shape of the furniture you are polishing (e.g. diagonal passes, figures of eight, etc.).
9 Store your rubber between sessions in a tight-lidded container with a splash of meths.

THE SECOND SESSION

You can if you wish stop completely at this stage. You will have achieved a low-key, open grained, low lustre, sealer-type French polish finish, which is both quick and effective.

Achieving a high gloss requires more work. First, gently stroke the surface with 600 grit wet-and-dry paper to remove any roughness. You may not notice any roughness, but if you rub one side of your tester with wet-and-dry and then rub your hand over both surfaces you will notice the difference.

Wipe off any dust with a clean rag and repeat the first day's session.

Work through the various passes in sequence and watch the shine build up. The more you polish the more it will shine. After more passes you will find that the surface will again become sticky. It is vital that this does not cause the rubber to stop, for the reasons explained earlier.

If this does happen you must allow the polish to dry overnight, rub it down with wet-and-dry until the blemish cannot be seen and start again.

To avoid such problems, stop when the surface becomes sticky, and leave it overnight before continuing, or, to prevent the stickiness from occurring, flick raw linseed oil on the surface (see Fig 15.14). The linseed oil will act as a lubricant for the rubber and will allow you to carry on polishing. Often it will allow you to polish even harder than normal, so increasing the burnishing action and the shine. Sometimes it may look a little smeary and lose a little of the shine, but this disappears as you continue to polish.

SPIRITING OFF

Allow the second session or sessions to dry overnight and then begin the final polish process. For this you will need a brand new rubber which is

Fig 15.14 Flick raw linseed oil on to the surface of the wood to prevent stickiness occurring.

charged with a small quantity of methylated spirit. Pour the meths into the cotton wool and squeeze the rubber so that the sole becomes almost dry to the touch. If it leaves a wet patch when squeezed hard against a dry piece of paper it is too wet. If it leaves a damp patch when squeezed hard, it is about right.

Dip your forefinger into the linseed oil and flick it over the polished surface. Wipe the excess from your finger with the sole of the rubber. Do this twice. Now hover above the wood practising your circular motion in mid-air, then lower the rubber until you reach the wood and apply light pressure to rub in a circular motion as you did when you applied the first pass. It will take a little time before the meths starts to soften the polish, and then the abrasive quality of the cloth will start to burnish the polish. As the shine begins to develop and the oil gets spread around, increase the pressure and the speed. This is the most strenuous part of the process and is best carried out in short, energetic bursts, and this is when the shine really begins to appear.

The spiriting technique is really an abrasive process. If you have any slight blemishes on the surface it is possible to rub them out of the polish with this technique. But beware: if the finish is too thin it is possible to rub right through the finish to the wood.

Spiriting done, apply a finishing touch in the form of a light application of wax, which should be buffed to a superlative shine. Although the polish is dry to the touch it will be at least a week before it goes rock hard. Do not, therefore, place anything heavy on the surface or it will mark.

If you choose to work on a large piece of furniture once you have gained more experience, as with other finishing techniques, break the surface into manageable sections and complete them one pass at a time.

COMMON PROBLEMS

There are a number of problems that can occur with this type of finish. Here are some of the commonest ones encountered by those new to the technique, and some remedies.

- The polish is too thick and cannot be applied thinly enough or evenly enough. Thin the polish with meths.
- There is too much polish on the rubber, making thin lines on the surface. Allow the polish to dry and cut back with wet-and-dry. Adjust the amount of polish in the rubber, or the amount of downward pressure.

Fig 15.15 The wrong way to hold the rubber. Always grip it close to the base of the twist (as shown in Fig 15.9), otherwise it will 'rock and roll'.

- Not enough polish is being applied to the edges or corners of the piece. Concentrate more upon these areas, or make some rogue passes as required.
- Rough patches appear as a result of the rubber going over freshly applied polish and sticking to it, or by stopping on the polish and redissolving it. Try not to get so close when butting up against the previous row of polish, and never, never stop the rubber on the surface.
- The rubber 'rocks and rolls' in the grip. This is due to it not being held close enough to the foot (see Fig 15.15). This causes the sides where the polish builds up to come into contact with the surface and spoil the finish. Hold the rubber firmly and close to the foot at all times.

- Scratches to the finish caused by dirt, grit or tears on the sole of the rubber. Check the sole frequently and if necessary, change rubbers.
- Somebody puts a hot cup of tea on the table within days of completion. Stay calm and remove the mark with rubbing compound or spirit off.

APPLYING NON-GLOSS FINISHES

If you would prefer a satin finish, after the second session of building up, instead of spiriting off, stroke the surface with fine-grade wire wool and thin wax. Make sure you only stroke with the grain. Do not scrub the finish as this will produce arc-shaped scratches and ruin the effect.

If you are looking for a matt finish, rub in the same way but use a little more pressure, and experiment with a coarser grade wire wool.

FRENCH POLISHING WITH A BRUSH

This is a relatively quick method of achieving a French polish finish on furniture, often used by the commercial French polisher to speed up the more time-consuming and superior rubber process. It would be beneficial to have read the preceding section before embarking on this technique.

French polish was applied with a brush for centuries before the rubber was invented, and using a brush remains the quickest way to achieve a finish with French polish.

The technique can also be combined with the traditional method, in order to speed that process up as you require.

PREPARATION

You can apply this finish with an ordinary decorator's brush, but it will be improved and made easier by using a special French polishing brush. These are known as 'flatties' and are designed especially for applying quick-drying finishes.

The difference between an ordinary brush and a flatty is best illustrated by viewing the two brushes from the side: the flatty is about three times thinner in this side dimension (see Fig 15.16). Unfortunately, these brushes are not widely available in DIY stores, but they can be found in some model

Fig 15.16 Here you can see the difference between a traditional decorator's brush (right) – designed to be used with slow-drying finishes such as oil paints and polyurethane varnishes – and a 'flatty', designed for use with quick-drying finishes such as French polish.

*Fig 15.17
Applying the
polish in quick,
even strokes, as
briskly as
possible, using a
'flatty'.*

and craft shops. Failing this, they can be ordered from trade supply houses (ask for a brush to apply French polish). Alternatively, have a go with an ordinary decorator's brush; many of my students have had great success with these.

APPLICATION

As with the rubber technique, do not try to apply polish in damp, cold or draughty surroundings. Mix your French polish in the usual way (50/50 with meths), then dip just the first 25% of your brush hair into this mix if you are using a flatty. Dip only 10% if you are using a decorator's brush.

Apply the polish in quick, even strokes as briskly as possible (see Fig 15.17). Do not splash the polish anywhere (if you do you've probably got too much on the brush), and work around the furniture systematically in the following way:

1 Dip the brush.
2 Apply the polish.
3 Brush out drips or runs.
4 Move on.

Do not spend hours lovingly stroking the finish out; remember the polish will dry quickly and as soon as this happens the brush will stick, leaving a drag mark. Just let the tips of the brush hairs come into contact with the surface.

The aim, as with the traditional technique, is to cover the surface with lots of very thin coats of polish as evenly as possible. Leave each application for 15 minutes to dry, lightly rub down with wet-and-dry and repeat. Subsequent coats will go on much more easily, and you will quickly build up a shine. After about four or five coats, allow the polish to dry overnight.

The next day, rub down and continue as before, still rubbing down lightly between each coat. When rubbing down, beware of the edges of the wood where it is possible to rub away the polish completely.

If you make a mistake and miss a drip or leave a drag mark, just allow it to dry hard, and rub it out with wet-and-dry.

INCREASING THE SHINE

Once you have built up what you consider to be a suitable finish, stop.

If you desire an even higher polish, proceed as follows.

Allow the polish to dry for seven days, and then, using a damp rag, rub burnishing cream into the polished finish (see Fig 15.18). Make sure you do not overdo it, particularly on the edges and the corners, as the cream is abrasive.

Soon you will see a high polish develop, and this process will also remove some of the garish quality sometimes associated with brushed French polish.

Next take a small brush dipped in some white spirit and use it to brush out any white powder deposits the burnishing cream has left in small crevices etc. Finally, wipe over with a coat of liquid wax and buff (see Chapter 13).

Fig 15.18 Burnishing cream will help to achieve a high polish. Photograph courtesy of Liberon Waxes Ltd.

An even higher shine can be achieved by using the same processs as that employed in the final stages of traditional French polishing: spiriting off (see page 116).

The brush technique is often used to polish areas that are difficult to access with a rubber, such as carved and fretted areas. Sometimes, table tops will be finished with a rubber, and the less visible legs with a brush.

COLOURING FRENCH POLISH

French polish can be coloured by adding a spirit stain to the brushing mix. In this way you can get a black (ebony) finish, a red (mahogany) finish, or any other coloured finish you desire. (See Chapter 12 on stains and Chapter 17 on ebonizing.)

OTHER RECIPES FOR FRENCH POLISH

THE QUICK AND EASY RECIPE

Fill the grain as described on page 72, build up a thick coating of polish

with a brush, apply the second session with a rubber, and then spirit off.

THE CRAFTSPERSON'S RECIPE

For the perfect finish, all coats are applied with a rubber, and the first coats are applied undiluted. The finish is always rubbed down between sessions with wet-and-dry. As the finish builds up, the polish is thinned down progressively. First 50/50 polish and meths, then 40/60, 30/70, 20/80, 10/90 and finally spirit off with 100% meths.

FURTHER INFORMATION

For further information on French polishing as part of the restoration process, please refer to:

- Chapter 8 on how to strip antique furniture sympathetically before repolishing.
- Chapters 5 and 11 on how to repair minor blemishes in French polish finishes.
- Chapter 11 on how to fill the grain in coarse woods before French polishing.

16
VARNISHES

Because the choice of polyurethane varnishes is so vast, it is useful to be aware of those elements common to all types.

- The method of application is the same for all polyurethane varnishes.
- All polyurethane varnishes are applied with a decorator's brush.
- Each coat takes between 4 and 12 hours to dry.
- All polyurethane varnishes emit a paint-type smell which lasts as long as the varnish takes to dry.
- Expect bare wood to require three coats of polyurethane varnish for a satisfactory finish.
- Uncoloured, clear polyurethane varnishes are usually the colour of golden treacle and are thinned, and their brushes cleaned, with white spirit (see Fig 16.1).
- Polyurethane varnishes are available in gloss, satin or matt finishes.
- Some are available specially formulated for outdoor use.
- Some are available with stains added to them, and usually take on the name of the stain; i.e. polyurethane varnish with a walnut stain will normally be known as a walnut varnish.

Fig 16.1 The thickness of polyurethane varnishes varies, but this gluey consistency is typical, and makes it more difficult to obtain a good looking finish. It will cover the wood quicker, but as your goal is quality, not speed, thin it down with white spirit every time.

▌ Correctly applied, polyurethane varnish creates an extremely beautiful finish. Badly applied it looks awful and can deteriorate (see Fig 16.2).

POSITIVE ASPECTS OF POLYURETHANE VARNISH

▌ It is hard wearing, scratch-resistant, heat- and water-resistant, alcohol-resistant.
▌ It is less brittle than other hard finishes and hence resistant to knocks and bangs.

▌ It will 'move' with the wood as the wood expands or contracts according to the seasons or changes in humidity.
▌ A flawless mirror-like shine is possible if correctly applied.

NEGATIVE ASPECTS OF POLYURETHANE VARNISH

▌ As I have said, if poorly applied it looks terrible.
▌ Inadequate application results in flaking off.
▌ The coloured varieties of the

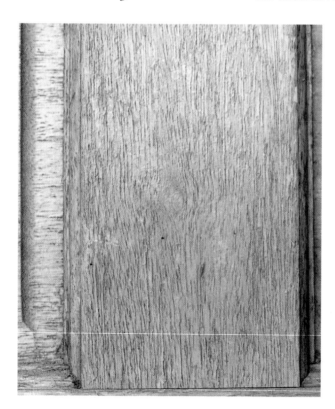

Fig 16.2
Deteriorating
polyurethane
varnish.

varnish tend to obscure the wood underneath and have a very muddied look to them. They are not recommended. Far better to use a separate stain applied directly to the wood before varnishing.

How to apply a gloss polyurethane varnish

PREPARATION

Polyurethane varnish has a long drying time, and as a result, there are many things which can go wrong. Minimizing the possibility of these is the first step to success.

Make sure you have an application area which is warm and dry: heat will help speed up the drying process. Do not varnish on days when there are large numbers of insects hatching, matching and dispatching all around you. Take the wind factor into account. You will need to have some windows open to aid drying and release fumes. Avoid being disturbed; get out the 'do not disturb' sign and put it to use.

If you are applying the varnish in a shed or garage, sweep the floor and dust the shelves before you begin, then allow 24 hours for the disturbed dust to settle. A vacuum cleaner is very useful to minimize the dust. Finally, lay some dust sheets or old newspaper down to protect the floor and keep floor dust at bay.

Always, always use a clean brush. Do not use a brush that has been used previously for painting, or any other function. No matter how well you think you have cleaned a used brush there will always be some dirt lurking among the bristles. Best to buy a new brush and reserve it for varnishing and nothing else.

For most jobs a 1½ or 2in (38 or 51mm) brush will do. Buy the best you can afford (you do not want the bristles of a cheap brush detaching themselves during varnishing and taking up residence in your otherwise dirt- and insect-free finish).

Before using your new brush for the first time, clean it in some warm water and washing up liquid to remove dust and hairs, then dry it on a clean cloth and varnish a scrap of clean cardboard or wood. Keep brushing until the varnish becomes a bit sticky. This will remove the loose hairs which inevitably reside in new (even expensive) brushes. Finally, clean the brush in white spirit, wrap some clingfilm or cooking foil around the bristles and store in a dust-free environment ready for use.

Before you begin, remember to raise the work to a comfortable height to prevent bending over.

You will also need:

■ A pot or jar with a neck wide enough to accept your brush.
■ White spirit.
■ Your chosen gloss varnish (always use new varnish – old varnish deteriorates).
■ Rubbing compound.
■ Wet-and-dry abrasive paper.
■ Old rags.
■ Wax polish.
■ Protective gloves.

APPLICATION

1 Stir the varnish slowly with a clean stick for 60 seconds. Do not shake or stir vigorously as you do not want any small air bubbles getting trapped in the varnish.

2 Pour some varnish into your wide-necked pot, to about halfway.

3 Thin the varnish with between 10 and 30% white spirit depending on the thickness of the varnish. Varnish should run off your brush easily; aim for the consistency of milk, and don't worry if it's a bit too thin – this is far better than too thick. (Non-drip varnishes should not be thinned in this way, but you can ease your path by dipping the first 25% of your brush in white spirit and shaking off the excess before dipping into the varnish.)

4 Only dip the first 25% of the brush bristles into the varnish to prevent excessive dripping (see Fig 16.3). Apply the first coat, working systematically around the work. Do not flit from one section to another. Work to a system and you will be less likely to miss a bit.

5 Now use a brush to spread the varnish as far as it will go. The

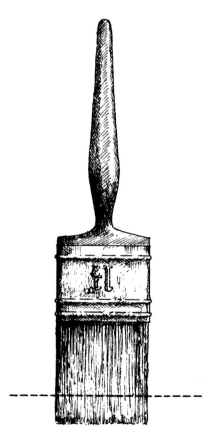

Fig 16.3 Only dip the first 25% of the bristles into the varnish.

more you can spread the varnish the less chance there will be of it dripping and (on non-horizontal surfaces) sagging as it dries. Pay particular attention to carved areas – do not let the varnish build up too thickly. If your project has been stained, your brush will pick up some of the stain from the wood as you apply the first coat. Therefore, apply the first coat over a stain with the minimum of brushing. Be quick and decisive, applying the varnish with the brush and then leaving it. In this way the wood and its stain will become sealed in, and the stain will not be picked up by the next coat of varnish.

6   Once the first coat has been applied to your satisfaction you must check to ensure there are no drips, runs, sags or sections which have been missed.

7   Leave the first coat to dry overnight and then lightly rub down with fine abrasive paper to remove all roughness from the surface of the finish. Beware; even if the surface does not look rough, it probably will be, in the same way as a French-polished finish (see Chapter 15). Be careful on the edges and corners of the project not to rub through to the wood. Any drips or blemishes can also be removed

at this stage by rubbing them down.

8   Wipe away any dust from the rubbing down with a clean rag dampened with white spirit.

This process can now be repeated. You will find that the second and subsequent coats will spread further as the varnish will not sink so readily into the wood. They will also dry more quickly.

As each coat is applied, a shine will begin to develop. Don't forget to rub down lightly between each coat. Apply as many coats as it takes to obtain the thickness of finish you require. If you thinned down the varnish as I advised and want to go for a mirror finish, I would suggest a minimum of five coats, but this will depend on the thickness of the varnish and the type of wood.

Now allow the finish to dry thoroughly – I recommend allowing seven days in a warm room.

THE FINAL STAGE

To achieve the mirror-finish, and prevent the varnish looking too garish, use rubbing compound to polish your project. The more you polish the more it will shine. Remember not to rub too hard on the edges and corners. This done, wash away any white powdery residue with a brushful of white spirit.

Lastly, rub over the work with a coat of thin wax polish (see Chapter 13), and polish up with a clean duster.

HOW TO APPLY A NON-GLOSS POLYURETHANE VARNISH

Such finishes can either be achieved by using a purpose-made satin varnish, or by reducing the gloss of a gloss varnish finish.

To reduce the gloss of a gloss varnish finish, do not leave the varnish to harden for seven days or apply any rubbing compound. Instead, leave the piece for two days and then go to work with some medium- or fine-grade wire wool and some beeswax. Rub the wax into the varnish with the wire wool, stroking with the grain, and then finish off with a light waxing. The more you stroke with the wire wool, the duller the finish will become. Do not scrub the wire wool backwards and forwards, but use the same action you would to stroke a cat (see Fig 16.4).

A ready-made satin varnish is applied in the same way as a gloss varnish, without the 'shining up' stages.

A matt finish is achieved with the use of a matt varnish, applied in the same way as gloss, but once again without the need for the rubbing compound or waxing stages.

COLOURING POLYURETHANE VARNISH

If you wish to colour the varnish for patching-in faded or worn areas, and for colouring fillers, add oil stain or artist's oil colour (see Chapter 12).

COMMON PROBLEMS

Most problems occur with polyurethane varnish when it is applied too thickly. Always apply many thin coats, allowing each to dry and rubbing down with wet-and-dry or fine-grade sandpaper in between each coat. A thin coat dries quicker than a thick coat, and this gives less time for dust and bugs to settle on it and get trapped. It is also less heavy, and therefore less prone to runs, drips and sagging.

Outdoor varnishes often break down and flake off after prolonged exposure, leaving bare wood. The wood is then bleached by the sun and becomes unsightly and difficult to repair. The best way to tackle such problems is to remove the deteriorated varnish with sandpaper, and patch up with thinned polyurethane varnish, Danish oil or oil from another country (see Chapter 14). This will protect the bare wood until you have time to strip and refinish.

CREATING A SATIN FINISH USING WIRE WOOL

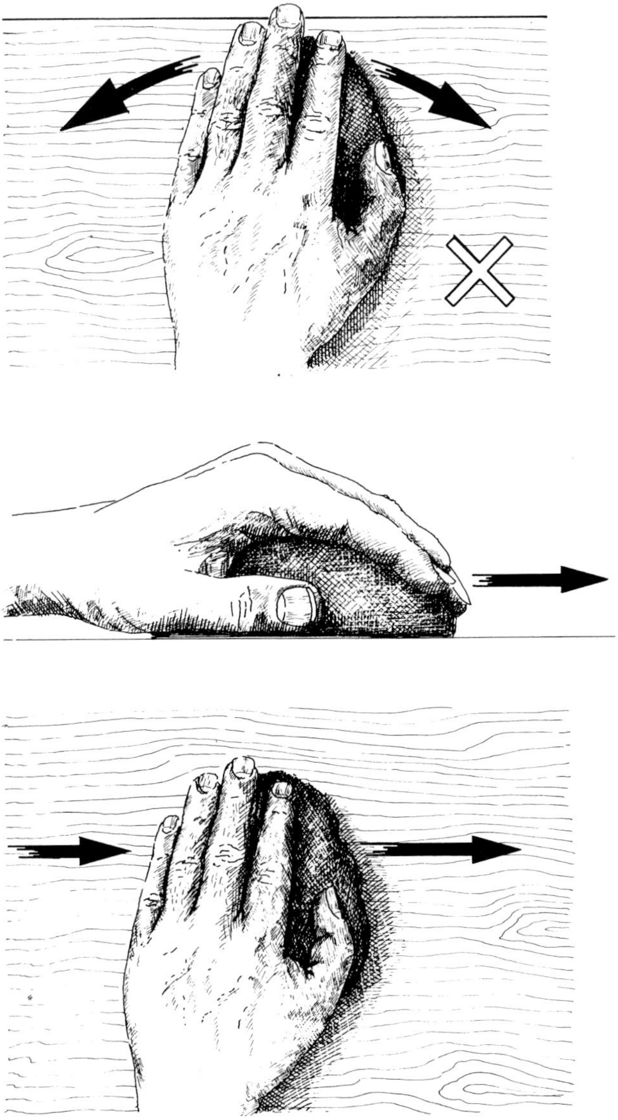

Fig 16.4 Do not stroke the wire wool backwards
and forwards; only with the grain.

Storing varnish

If you wish to store varnish for any length of time, push the lid firmly into place and stand the can upside down for 30 minutes. This will seal the lid in place and prevent a skin forming.

WATER-BASED VARNISHES

Unlike most wood finishes, whose solvent is meths (French polish), turpentine (wax), or white spirit (polyurethane varnish), water-based finishes have harmless water as their solvent. This has a number of important advantages.

Advantages

- Environmentally friendly.
- Quick drying (between 10 and 30 minutes depending on make and ambient conditions), to a crystal-clear film.
- Easily applied with an ordinary decorator's brush.
- Does not yellow with age (very helpful when dealing with light-coloured woods).
- No unpleasant smell during application.
- Non-flammable.
- Non-toxic.
- No risk of breathing problems in the user.
- Hard-wearing.
- Resistant to alcohol and boiling water.

The primary disadvantage with water-based varnishes is the fact that they will tend to raise the grain of the wood because of their water content. There are two ways to deal with this problem.

First, wet the grain of the bare wood prior to finishing, causing it to raise, allow the wood to dry, and sand down thoroughly with fine-grade abrasive paper. When the wood is made wet again the grain will stay flat. Do not use this method on veneered surfaces, as you are liable to damage the veneer.

For veneers, apply a thin coat of varnish, allow to dry and then very carefully rub down. Always guard against over-wetting.

Alternatively you could consider using the naturally decorative qualities of raised grain. This works very well on nicely figured woods such as pine, oak and elm. Raise the grain of the wood as described above (if need be, wet the wood several times), and when dry, varnish over the top. The result is a natural 'textured' surface that can, with a little luck, look quite stunning. However, success does depend on the type of wood used, and a little luck.

PREPARATION

Make sure the ambient conditions are right before you begin. Avoid application in damp, cold, dusty or windy conditions, or in high humidity. Avoid direct sunlight or heat during application, or the finish will become sticky, the brush will drag and the final finish be spoiled.

Different manufacturers provide different instructions on how to apply water-based varnish, and these general guidelines should give you a good idea of what is involved and how to get the best results.

If applicable, thin the varnish with its solvent: water. Not all varnishes need thinning. If in doubt, contact the manufacturer for advice. Use a new brush to apply the varnish, having cleaned it thoroughly in warm soapy water and allowed it to dry thoroughly. Do not use an old brush.

When liquid, water-based varnishes are a milky-white colour, but they dry clear (see Fig 16.5). They are available for indoor and outdoor use, and also as a special flooring-quality finish.

All manufacturers carry gloss, satin and matt finishes, and many supply water-based stains, tints and paints.

APPLICATION

1 Apply the first coat as thinly as possible to the bare wood and brush it out quickly before it becomes tacky.
2 Allow to dry.
3 Rub down any raised grain.
4 Wipe off any dust with a damp cloth. No further raised grain should now occur as you proceed.
5 Apply further coats in the same way, rubbing down lightly with fine abrasive paper between coats to remove imperfections.
6 Stop when you have a good build-up of varnish. Areas of high wear such as table tops will benefit from an extra one or two coats to aid durability.

Fig 16.5 Water-based varnishes are a milky-white colour when liquid, but dry to a clear finish.

7 Wait for seven days before burnishing (if required) with rubbing compound to achieve a mirror-like finish (see page 127), or treating it with wire wool to dull it or enhance a matt or satin finish (see pages 128–9).

If your project has been stained the brush will tend to pick up the stain as you work. A way round this is to use a trigger-operated garden spray (see Fig 16.6). Fill the spray with the varnish and spray the work methodically, giving a good coating of finish to one area at a time. Wipe off excess drips straight away with a cotton cloth, being careful not to interfere too much with the stained surface. Then move on to the next part.

It usually takes two or three coats from the spray before the stain is sealed in, and then you can revert to a brush, or, if you prefer, continue applying subsequent coats with the spray.

Job done, cleaning your brush is easy; run it under warm soapy water and dry with a cloth. Never allow your brush to harden between coats; either wash it out or keep it in a tumbler of water.

RESTORATION

Repairing and restoring a water-based varnish is a simple job. Just rub it down with a fine abrasive paper and recoat it. A well-used piece will benefit from cleaning down the surface with white spirit to remove grease, dirt and wax, before rubbing down and recoating.

I advise you to try water-based varnishes, as they are so convenient, particularly if you are working in your house and have to be mindful of the needs and feelings of others. The safety factor also comes into play here; if you have children or pets, water-based finishes can cause a lot fewer headaches, being so environmentally friendly and super-safe.

Fig 16.6 You can use an ordinary garden spray for applying any water-based finish, or reviver.

17
EBONIZING

For the uninitiated, ebonizing is the craft of making ordinary, run-of-the-mill wood look like ebony. This is the furniture restorer's equivalent of the medieval alchemist transforming lead into gold.

Ebonizing can be divided into two distinct areas: first, the highly skilled efforts of the true craftsperson who endeavours to copy exactly the look of the finest-grade ebony cabinetwork; second, the less professional method, which should most properly be called staining the wood jet black. This method is very useful, and, when done with skill, produces a beautiful finish. It is a little easier than the orthodox method because the process is not so concerned with the finer details of ebonizing such as copying the grain structure of ebony, or disguising the true nature of the wood. What follows encompasses both types of finish, enabling you to decide which is best for your project.

A LIFESAVER FINISH

These finishes have three marvellous and very important properties.

- They look very exotic and beautiful.
- They are easy to achieve.
- They are able to cover up or disguise all manner of blemishes and imperfections which would otherwise ruin a perfectly usable piece of furniture (see Fig 17.1).

Fig 17.1 The extent of this burn mark makes ebonizing a wise technique to apply in restoring this piano.

It has to be said at this stage that an ebony finish will not always look right on every piece of furniture. To the tutored eye, true ebony furniture is usually slender, fragile and elegant in style. This style is a reflection of the wood's rarity and the small sections that it is naturally available in (see Fig 17.2). If you apply this finish to rugged furniture it may look slightly 'wrong', but there is no harm in experimenting. These are just 'awareness guides' to help you understand this finish's finer points.

THE TRADITIONAL EBONIZING TECHNIQUE

The first essential for proper ebonizing is a close-grained wood. The old-time craftsmen used to

Fig 17.2 This graceful little table is an ideal candidate for ebonizing.

employ a variety of different types of wood to copy the ebony look. However, since you are not making the furniture, only restoring it, this aspect is beyond your control. But it is worth knowing that of the common furniture-making woods, beech, close-grained mahogany and fruit woods such as apple, lime and pear are ideal candidates for the enthusiastic ebonizer.

If you have very open-grained wood, you can always fill the grain (see Chapter 11). Without a filler, open woods will not pass muster as an ebonized finish, but will still look very attractive with jet-black finishes.

You will need:

- Black spirit stain.
- French polish.
- Meths.
- A French-polishing brush (see Chapter 15).
- Wire wool.
- Liquid wax.
- A soft buffing cloth.

Black spirit stain is best bought in powder form and mixed to your desired strength with methylated spirit. You can buy spirit stain in liquid form, but it is often not strong enough to turn the wood jet black.

For something the size of a chair you will need approximately a teaspoonful of powder. To this add half a pint (264mls) of meths. Test this on the wood by painting the stain on with a brush. It should totally obliterate the colour of the wood and turn it charcoal black. If the mix is too strong then a black powder will be left on the surface of the wood. If it is too weak then the colour of the wood will not be completely obscured and will look greyish blue.

When you have achieved the correct strength, paint the rest of the project with the stain. Try not to handle the furniture too much at this stage, as you are likely to end up looking like an overworked chimney sweep.

Now mix some black French polish by pouring the required amount of French polish into a wide-brimmed jar and adding the same quantity of black spirit stain.

APPLICATION

Apply three coats of this finish with a brush as described in Chapter 15. Rub down very lightly between coats, being careful not to rub away stain at the corners and edges. If you do remove stain, apply some neat stain to the area with an artist's brush and polish over the top.

The crucial test of a good coating of stain is to view the project in bright sunlight. So when you have put your first coat of polish on, take the piece out of doors at midday for an inspection. Better still, take the day off, put it in the back of the car and take it to the park – the rest will do you good. You may be surprised at how much is disclosed by pure sunlight, and how much is hidden by artificial lighting.

When you have built up a thick enough surface and it is looking glossy, leave it overnight to dry. Next morning, stroke the surface over with fine-grade wire wool and a liquid wax (see Chapter 13).

Be sure to stroke the surface *with* the grain and keep the stroking

action straight. Do not scrub in a windscreen wiper motion, as this will lead to curved scratches that will ruin the ebony grain effect.

When you have finished, buff with a soft rag. After this you will undoubtedly spot areas you have missed and that are too shiny; go back and rub with wire wool a bit more. Always beware of rubbing too hard on edges and corners; if you do, touch in with some black French polish.

All the while you are involved in this process, try to keep in mind the type of finish you are trying to

Fig 17.3 By rubbing black paint into the wood you can create a rich deep black stain, which can then be overcoated with satin polyurethane varnish for a fine finish. (Incidentally, you can do this with any colour paint, so if you can't find the correct colour stain, experiment with rubbing paints into the wood.)

Fig 17.4 You can easily patch up ebonized furniture with a black marker pen.

achieve: very satiny, very hard and very black.

If you prefer a hard-wearing finish, try staining the wood with the same spirit dyes and then adding the remaining stain to some satin finish cellulose lacquer.

STAINING BLACK WITHOUT EBONIZING

If you just want to stain your project black and then coat it with a finish, you can choose any of the finishes so far described in this book. One very good method is to rub black gloss oil paint thinned with a little white spirit into the wood and then overcoat with some satin polyurethane varnish (see Fig 17.3).

The care and maintenance of an ebonized finish depends on the type of finish you apply over the stain. However, if you happen to chip or scratch the finish so that the lighter base wood shows through, you can repair the blemish with a black spirit marker pen by rubbing it over the offending area (see Fig 17.4). Scratches can be filled with black wax or black French polish.

18
PAINTED FINISHES

Paint is the perfect way to transform, say, a drab chair into an attractive chair. If you are fed up with me waffling on about grain structures, the natural beauty of wood and patinas, have a go with this finish.

STYLES OF
PAINTED FINISH

There are two distinct types of painted furniture. The first are those which require a little practice and perhaps the ability to paint in a realistic manner, such as *trompe-l'oeil*, marbling and graining. The second are those painting skills that just need good instruction and are easily managed by someone new to painting. These are the techniques addressed in this chapter.

ANOTHER LIFESAVER
FINISH

Painted finishes, like ebonizing and black staining, are a 'lifesaver finish'. Every blemish known to man, no matter how bizarre, can be obliterated under a beautiful coat of artistically applied paint. This finish also allows you a great deal of artistic and creative freedom.

CHOOSING THE COLOUR

One of the biggest problems with painted finishes is choosing the colour scheme. Colour is notoriously difficult to choose, and I hope to make it easy for you. If you are going to use the instructions that follow, you will need two colours: one is white (half the problem solved) and the other should suit the colour scheme of the room in which the painted piece will eventually live. Choose a colour that is the same as one of the major colours in that room – the colour of the carpet; the walls; the ceiling; the curtains, even the rest of the furniture. Try taking some colour swatches (available wherever you buy paint) to the room and sit there for a while contemplating. Take stock of what is already there and try to make a match. If you think you may have found a colour but are still not sure, go and buy a small pot of it, apply it to a sheet of card or hardboard, and stand this in the room for perusal.

Sometimes you won't know where the piece will end up, so you can let yourself go and pander to your creative whims. If you don't like it, you can always paint over it!

For the purposes of this chapter I shall assume you have chosen dark blue as your colour to add to your pot of white paint.

CHOOSING YOUR PAINT

Decorator's oil paint is slow drying, and its thinners and brush cleaner is white spirit. It is also available in satin or matt finishes, and in a huge range of colours. If you can't find the colour you want, it can be mixed for you by many stores. This is the paint to use when painting furniture.

MIXING PAINT

Here is how to make a perfect colour match. Decant some of the white paint into a screw-top container, add a teaspoonful of the blue and stir thoroughly for three or four minutes (see Fig 18.1). This will produce a light blue that will harmonize perfectly with the dark blue. The lighter colour will be applied first and will cover the whole piece, so make sure you mix enough.

Once you have coated the furniture in light blue, mix some more dark blue into the light blue, thus creating a mid-blue. The mid-blue and the navy blue will be used to create the 'decoration'.

The same principle of mixing a colour with white to produce a lighter shade produces a good colour combination with all colours; try it and see.

Fig 18.1 White and blue paints decanted into jars prior to mixing.

APPLICATION

First strip the furniture back to the bare wood (see Chapter 7). If it is cabinet furniture, i.e. it has drawers or cupboard space, decide at this stage if you want to paint the insides of these areas. If you do (a contrasting colour in these areas can produce stunning results), you will need to strip these areas as well.

When you have finished, fill any holes and mend any broken bits, then rub the wood down with medium-grade sandpaper to leave a smooth surface (see Fig 18.2).

You will quickly discover, if you do not know already, that paint has a special way of finding its way on to every conceivable part of your anatomy, and thinned paint is easily flicked off the bristles of your brush to land anywhere up to a five-mile radius. So always protect the surfaces surrounding your work with newspaper, and try to protect yourself by wearing old clothes. Have some white spirit and cloths to hand to clean off paint. The following will help you to stay reasonably paint-free.

▮ Decant the paint into a shallow container so that it is no more than ½in (13mm) deep. This will stop the brush sinking into the paint and coating the handle as well as the bristles, and will save you wiping the bristles on the rim of the can, causing drips to run down the outside.
▮ Only dip the tip of the brush into the paint.
▮ Keep the handle scrupulously clean.
▮ Keep your hands clean.

Fig 18.2 This little cabinet was found in a skip. It has been stripped, the damaged top replaced with some plywood, and new doorknobs added. It is now ready to be brought back to useful life by the application of a painted finish.

▌ Wipe up spills, drips and runs as they occur.

Before you begin painting, you may find it helpful to think of paint as polyurethane varnish with pigments added, and read Chapter 16, which describes some of the finer points of varnish (paint) application in detail.

Now you can begin painting, as follows.

1   Thin down the first coat with 10% white spirit, and apply it to your project, as ever working methodically around the piece.

This coat is intended to soak deep into the wood. This is important as the next coat will attach itself to this one, and needs a good 'anchor'. Otherwise, in years to come, the paint may flake.

2   After 15 minutes, check for drips and runs, and wipe any off with a cloth dampened with white spirit.

Fig 18.3 Three coats of light blue paint later, the cabinet is transformed, and could be left like this, or some painted embellishments added.

3 Leave the piece to dry overnight.
4 Rub down with wet-and-dry abrasive paper, and apply the next coat in a similar way to the first, but not thinned. Three or four coats should suffice.

The secret to this type of finish is the rubbing down between coats; this is just as important as carefully applying the paint.

You should now have a light blue piece of furniture. You can leave it like that if you wish (see Fig 18.3), or proceed by applying some dark blue.

I limited the darker colour on the cabinet to some well-defined areas. I drew a border in pencil around the doors and top of the piece, and filled them with the dark blue paint using an artist's brush (see Fig 18.4).

For the cloudy-looking areas I decided to use a technique known as 'ragging on'. This involves screwing up a rag of cotton cloth

Fig 18.4 Decorative borders serve to further enhance the piece. You can see I also opted to paint the knobs gold, but the dark blue would have looked equally good.

Fig 18.5 To make the pad for 'ragging on', fold and roll up a cotton cloth into a rose-like shape, until you have a pad that leaves a satisfactory print.

and then using the texture and the folds of the cloth to print a mid-blue colour over the light blue (see Fig 18.5). This mid-blue is achieved by mixing another teaspoon of dark blue into the light blue. Test your print on a piece of paper first to establish how hard you have to push and how much paint you need to use (see Fig 18.6). It will take a little experimenting before you get the right mix of paint and pressure.

Fig 18.6 Test the pad on a spare sheet of paper before applying it to the furniture.

When you think it is about right, transfer to the furniture. Protect with newspaper any areas you do not want painted, and start printing.

Once the first coat has dried you can apply another one on top, so building up the depth of the decoration. If you overdo it, rag on a little of the lighter blue to mingle with the mid-blue and break up the darker colour.

When you are happy with your handiwork, allow the piece to dry overnight, then give it a protective top coat to seal everything in. If you have used a lighter colour scheme, as in my example, I suggest you use two or three coats of white French polish or satin water-based varnish, as these finishes do not discolour with age. Alternatively, you can use satin polyurethane varnish, but I only use this with darker colour schemes, as it does tend to yellow with age (see Fig 18.7).

Fig 18.7 The finished cabinet.

GLOSSARY

ANILINE DYES
Variation on spirit dyes.

BITE
The ability of a stain to penetrate into the wood.

BURNISHING CREAM
Paste used to polish hard substances.

CABINET FURNITURE
Furniture with drawers and/or doors.

CABRIOLE LEGS
A type of curved leg design much used in old furniture.

CAR RUBBING COMPOUND
Burnishing cream prepared specifically for use on cars.

CHIPBOARD
Man-made wood composed of compressed wood chips.

CHIPPENDALE
Famous 18th-century master cabinetmaker.

CLAW HAMMER
Special type of hammer incorporating device for removing nails.

DISCLOSER STAIN
Thin stain used to highlight blemishes prior to use.

DOWELS
Rods made of wood.

EMULSION PAINT
Water-based paint much used in home decoration.

FORMICA
Man-made plastic veneer often used in food preparation areas.

FRETWORK
Decorative technique of cutting through thin wooden sections of wood to create a pattern.

GRAINING
Imitation of various wood grains using paint.

HACKSAW
Saw with very fine teeth used to cut metals.

HARDBOARD
Thin man-made board composed of compressed wood dust.

LEACH OUT
Drain out slowly.

LIGHT FAST
Will not fade in strong light.

LIPPINGS
Solid wood often used around the edge of veneered wood.

MARBLING
Imitation of marble using paint.

METHYLATED SPIRIT
Alcohol that has been denatured by the addition of methanol and pyridine and a violet dye. Also known as meths.

OAK PANELLING
Wall decoration composed of squares of oak wood.

PIGMENTS
Powders used to colour paint (amongst other things).

PLASTER OF PARIS
White powder that hardens when mixed with water.

PLASTICINE
A clay substitute used by artists and craftspeople.

PLYWOOD
Layers of veneer stuck together to make a board.

ROGUE PASSES
Unscheduled passes in French polishing, intended to fill in where scheduled passes miss.

SIDEBOARD
Piece of furniture traditionally used to store cutlery.

SOLID WOOD
Wood in its natural state, i.e. not veneered or man-made.

SPIRIT MARKER PEN
Pen with fibre tip and spirit-based ink.

STABLE WOOD
Wood known for its ability not to warp or move.

STAY
Hinge used to stop lids of boxes opening too far.

SUEDE BRUSH
Small brush with wire bristles.

TROMPE L'OEIL
Painted effect designed to deceive the eye.

METRIC CONVERSION TABLE

INCHES TO MILLIMETRES AND CENTIMETRES						
mm = millimetres cm = centimetres						
inches	mm	cm	inches	cm	inches	cm
$1/8$	3	0.3	9	22.9	30	76.2
$1/4$	6	0.6	10	25.4	31	78.7
$3/8$	10	1.0	11	27.9	32	81.3
$1/2$	13	1.3	12	30.5	33	83.8
$5/8$	16	1.6	13	33.0	34	86.4
$3/4$	19	1.9	14	35.6	35	88.9
$7/8$	22	2.2	15	38.1	36	91.4
1	25	2.5	16	40.6	37	94.0
$1 1/4$	32	3.2	17	43.2	38	96.5
$1 1/2$	38	3.8	18	45.7	39	99.1
$1 3/4$	44	4.4	19	48.3	40	101.6
2	51	5.1	20	50.8	41	104.1
$2 1/2$	64	6.4	21	53.3	42	106.7
3	76	7.6	22	55.9	43	109.2
$3 1/2$	89	8.9	23	58.4	44	111.8
4	102	10.2	24	61.0	45	114.3
$4 1/2$	114	11.4	25	63.5	46	116.8
5	127	12.7	26	66.0	47	119.4
6	152	15.2	27	68.6	48	121.9
7	178	17.8	28	71.1	49	124.5
8	203	20.3	29	73.7	50	127.0

ABOUT THE AUTHOR

Kevin Jan Bonner is an artist, designer, craftsman and teacher. After studying sculpture at art college, he started his own craft/design workshop, specializing in the design and manufacture of award-winning wooden toys. He has also spent many years teaching art and craft subjects at adult education institutes. He lives in North London.

INDEX

BOOKS

Carving Birds and Beasts . . . . .GMC Publications
Faceplate Turning . . . . .GMC Publications
Practical Tips for Turners and Carvers . . . . .GMC Publications
Practical Tips for Woodturners . . . . .GMC Publications
Useful Woodturning Projects . . . . .GMC Publications
Woodturning Techniques . . . . .GMC Publications
Woodworkers' Career and Educational Source Book . . . . .GMC Publications
Woodworking Plans and Projects . . . . .GMC Publications
40 More Woodworking Plans and Projects . . . . .GMC Publications
Green Woodwork . . . . .Mike Abbott
Easy to Make Dolls' House Accessories . . . . .Andrea Barham
Making Little Boxes from Wood . . . . .John Bennett
Woodturning Masterclass . . . . .Tony Boase
Furniture Restoration and Repair for Beginners . . . . .Kevin Jan Bonner
Woodturning Jewellery . . . . .Hilary Bowen
The Incredible Router . . . . .Jeremy Broun
Electric Woodwork . . . . .Jeremy Broun
Woodcarving: A Complete Course . . . . .Ron Butterfield
Making Fine Furniture: Projects . . . . .Tom Darby
Restoring Rocking Horses . . . . .Clive Green & Anthony Dew
Make Your Own Dolls' House Furniture . . . . .Maurice Harper
Practical Crafts: Seat Weaving . . . . .Ricky Holdstock
Multi-centre Woodturning . . . . .Ray Hopper
Complete Woodfinishing . . . . .Ian Hosker
Practical Crafts: Woodfinishing Handbook .Ian Hosker
Woodturning: A Source Book of Shapes . . . . .John Hunnex
Illustrated Woodturning Techniques . . . . .John Hunnex
Making Shaker Furniture . . . . .Barry Jackson
Upholstery: A Complete Course . . . . .David James
Upholstery Techniques and Projects . . . . .David James
The Uplolsterer's Pocket Reference Book . . . . .David James
Designing and Making Wooden Toys . . . . .Terry Kelly
Making Dolls' House Furniture . . . . .Patricia King
Making Victorian Dolls' House Furniture . . . . .Patricia King
Making and Modifying Woodworking Tools . . . . .Jim Kingshott
The Workshop . . . . .Jim Kingshott
Sharpening: The Complete Guide . . . . .Jim Kingshott
Sharpening Pocket Reference Book . . . . .Jim Kingshott
Turning Wooden Toys . . . . .Terry Lawrence
Making Board, Peg and Dice Games . . . . .Jeff & Jennie Loader
Making Wooden Toys and Games . . . . .Jeff & Jennie Loader
Bert Marsh: Woodturner . . . . .Bert Marsh
The Complete Dolls' House Book . . . . .Jean Nisbett
The Secrets of the Dolls' House Makers . . . . .Jean Nisbett
Wildfowl Carving, Volume 1 . . . . .Jim Pearce
Wildfowl Carving, Volume 2 . . . . .Jim Pearce

VIDEOS

MAGAZINES

WOODTURNING   WOODCARVING   BUSINESSMATTERS

All these publications are available through bookshops and newsagents,
or may be ordered by post from the publishers at:

**Castle Place, 166 High Street, Lewes, East Sussex BN7 1XU
Telephone (01273) 477374, Fax (01273) 478606**

Credit card orders are accepted

PLEASE WRITE OR PHONE FOR A FREE CATALOGUE